Elections: A Very Short Introduction

VERY SHORT INTRODUCTIONS are for anyone wanting a stimulating and accessible way into a new subject. They are written by experts, and have been translated into more than 45 different languages.

The series began in 1995, and now covers a wide variety of topics in every discipline. The VSI library currently contains over 750 volumes—a Very Short Introduction to everything from Psychology and Philosophy of Science to American History and Relativity—and continues to grow in every subject area.

Very Short Introductions available now:

Available soon:

For more information visit our website

www.oup.com/vsi/

L. Sandy Maisel and Jennifer A. Yoder

ELECTIONS

A Very Short Introduction

OXFORD
UNIVERSITY PRESS

OXFORD
UNIVERSITY PRESS

Oxford University Press is a department of the University of Oxford.
It furthers the University's objective of excellence in research, scholarship,
and education by publishing worldwide. Oxford is a registered trade mark of
Oxford University Press in the UK and in certain other countries.

Published in the United States of America by Oxford University Press
198 Madison Avenue, New York, NY 10016, United States of America.

Library of Congress Cataloging-in-Publication Data

Names: Maisel, Louis Sandy, 1945– author. | Yoder, Jennifer A., author.
Title: Elections : a very short introduction / L. Sandy Maisel, Jennifer A. Yoder.
Description: New York, NY : Oxford University Press, 2024. |
Series: Very short introductions | Includes bibliographical references and index.
Identifiers: LCCN 2024004611 (print) | LCCN 2024004612 (ebook) |
ISBN 9780197645758 (paperback) | ISBN 9780197645765 (epub) |
Subjects: LCSH: Elections. | Representative government and representation. |
Comparative government.
Classification: LCC JF1001 .M18 2024 (print) | LCC JF1001 (ebook) |
DDC 324.6—dc23/eng/20240222
LC record available at https://lccn.loc.gov/2024004611
LC ebook record available at https://lccn.loc.gov/2024004612

Integrated Books International, United States of America

To Patrice Franko and Greg Bazakas

Contents

List of illustrations

Acknowledgments

One inevitably incurs many debts in writing a book such as this
one. In a somewhat unusual manner, we want to start by thanking
each other. We have been colleagues and friends for a quarter
century, but we have never worked together on a project like this
one. Suffice it to say that we learned from each other, that we
benefited from our differing perspectives, and that we remain
friends.

Since the onset of COVID-19, Maisel has been honored to
participate in a weekly virtual seminar run by Stanford political
scientist David Brady. This book benefited immensely from those
conversations, and thanks are due to Brady, Bruce Cain,
Mo Fiorina, David Kennedy, Keith Krehbiel, and Doug Rivers
from Stanford; Roberto D'Alimonte and Sergio Fabbrini (Luiss
School of Government, Italy); John Ferejohn (NYU School of
Law); Denis Lecorne (Sciences Po, France); Gillian Peele (Oxford
University, England); and the most academic journalist any of us
knows, David Shribman, executive editor emeritus, *Pittsburgh
Post-Gazette*. We especially want to thank those seminar
participants and Helen Irving (University of Sydney, Australia)
and Steve Neumeister, who read and commented on an earlier
draft of this manuscript. We also are indebted to Lauren Gervais,
our Colby College research assistant on this project, and to Nancy
Toff, our editor; Ponneelan Moorthy, the project manager; and to

Peter Jaskowiak, our excellent copy editor at Oxford University Press, for their help in defining this project and seeing it through to fruition.

Finally, this book is dedicated from Sandy Maisel to Patrice Franko and from Jennifer Yoder to Greg Bazakas. Patrice is not only Sandy's loving wife, but a partner in all that I do; she knows me inside and out—and inspires me to do what I do. That has been especially important as I enter retirement—as she knows that retirement does not mean stopping for me; she has made my life complete for 30 years and will do so for many to come. Greg deserves thanks for being a dedicated partner, careful listener, and prudent adviser. His patience and his *joie de vivre* have made all the difference.

Elections

Preface

We were colleagues in the Government Department at Colby College for 25 years, until Maisel's retirement in 2021. Maisel specializes in American politics and has written extensively on American political parties and elections. Yoder is a comparativist, specializing in German politics and society and the politics of the European integration; her writing focuses on memory, politics, and identity. Our teaching and research interests have drawn us to examine the roles of institutions and rules and how they affect politics in different countries and different American states.

This project began as a proposal from Maisel to Oxford University Press to write a VSI on electoral rules. Nancy Toff, who edited Maisel's earlier VSI on American political parties and elections, suggested that the idea had merit, but that it would be much more interesting with a comparative perspective. Maisel agreed but noted he did not have that expertise—and thus a collaboration was born.

We began to think about this book shortly after the 2020 American presidential election, in the context of a deeply troubling electoral process. Never before in American history—not at the nation's inception, not during the Civil War, not during the Communist witch hunt in the 1950s, not when elections were agonizingly close as they were in 1960 and again in 2000—has a losing presidential candidate failed to concede to the winner. But that is exactly what Donald Trump did. And the flaws in the American electoral process were revealed for everyone to see.

We saw discontent among American citizens and a questioning of how the nation had arrived at such a state. And we began to look more deeply. The questions that drove our study were basic: What were the flaws that the 2020 election revealed? Why did they exist? And of special interest to us, were there lessons that American politicians and political reformers could learn from other countries that could be applied to the United States? If so, what were they?

Obviously, elections are multifaceted. At the macro level, countries differ from each other because of their constitutional designs and party systems. These are interrelated, but not necessarily determinative of each other. They differ regarding who can vote, how they vote, for whom they vote, and whether they vote. They differ in terms of how elections are administered. All of these have implications for the results of the electoral process, for who is elected, for how citizens relate to their elected officials, for the kinds of governing institutions that exist in a polity, and for the kinds of policies that are adopted. We quickly understood that the task we laid out for ourselves was no small one—and that covering it in the confines of a Very Short Introduction would not be easy.

But it has been fruitful for us. Writing this book enabled us to separate out those aspects of the electoral process that are fundamental to free, fair, open, and transparent elections and those that are peripheral. We have tried to separate our preferences—and ours are not always the same—from those aspects of elections that are fundamental. And mostly we have tried to encourage readers to think about their own views of the electoral process in their home country in a new way—not simply to understand what happens in elections, but to examine what the implications are of the ways in which elections are organized and run, to think about the values they believe should be expressed through the electoral process, and whether that with which they are most familiar can be improved.

Americans take great pride in their electoral process. As we were concluding this project, however, the Electoral Integrity Project, an academic research project based at Harvard University and Sydney University, released its 2022 report that rated the electoral integrity of the American electoral system 59th worldwide—and last among liberal democracies. There is no pride in that—and our hope is that the analysis in this book gives readers, especially American readers, food for thought about electoral reform.

But there are no panaceas, and reform that might be desirable is not always politically possible. As we finish writing this book, the January 6th Committee of the US House of Representatives has released its report on the aftermath of the 2020 election—and all of the problems that dreadful day revealed with the way in which Americans elect their president. But at the same time, Israel held its fifth national election in three years, because their system has not produced a government that can be sustained; Brazil's president, Jair Bolsonaro, stoked fears about election fraud in the run-up to general elections in his country, and his followers threatened the kinds of disruptions seen in Washington; and voters in Kenya voiced skepticism of the candidate selection process and their relatively new electronic voting system. We could easily draw on other examples—as democracies worldwide struggle to meet their citizens' needs.

Our hope in this book is to raise questions about the process for citizens in many countries. Electoral rules and processes are not exciting; they do not draw the fervor of a country's citizens, but they do lead to important decisions and choices with critical implications for citizens of any nation, and thus deserve all of our attention.

Chapter 1
Elections around the world

Most citizens have a basic understanding of how elections work in their own country, but they do not think much about the mechanisms through which elections function, especially if they follow the normal patterns. To use an illustration from the United States, American voters did not think much about how their president was elected following most of the elections at the end of the twentieth century; the person who received the most votes simply became president. Then, in 2000, Al Gore won the most votes, but George W. Bush won the election—after the Supreme Court intervened during the counting of votes in Florida and awarded that state's electoral votes to Bush. Hardly a normal election, the Bush-Gore contest caused Americans to ask questions about the process through which their national leader was chosen. Why were there challenges surrounding the counting of votes—the infamous "hanging chads"—in one state and not in others? How could the winner of the popular vote not win in the Electoral College? And why did the highest court in the country get involved in the determination of the winner?

Again in 2016, the winner of the popular vote in the US presidential election did not win the majority of the Electoral College votes, allowing Donald Trump to prevail over Hillary Clinton. Voters again had questions about the outcome. And certainly nothing was normal about the election of 2020, including the way in which the votes were counted and the losing incumbent's refusal to accept the results. Understandably, Americans have come to question the process through which their elections are run. Most may not understand the nuances of the process, but they are sure they do not like what they see.

When most elections in modern democracies produce obvious winners, citizens in those countries accept the result and, by implication, the process through which the result was achieved. But what about when the voting does not produce a result that is so apparent? Elections in Belgium have produced highly fragmented results, making it difficult to form governing coalitions. In 2010, it took 541 days after the elections to negotiate a new Belgian government. After the coalition government broke down in 2018, it took two years to form a government. Between 2019 and 2022, Israelis went to the polls five times, because none of the first four elections produced a stable governing coalition.

These situations demonstrate the significance of elections for governing, but, even more fundamentally, they point to the importance of understanding how and why elections function as they do. What difference do electoral rules make? What is the range of possible election systems? And how might reforms to election rules strengthen the principles that an electorate deems most important?

The most important reason to study electoral rules is that they often impact the way in which an election is conducted, the result of that election, and the ability of citizens to effect policy change through the electoral process. Elections determine who will hold public office and who will have the power to govern. They connect citizens to those they choose to make decisions on their behalf and to regulate their behavior. Yet not all elections in democracies are alike, and not all elections accomplish this task equally well. The rules of the game are not neutral, but most citizens—and most politicians—are familiar only with the system in which they function. Anything else is alien—and often viewed as inferior and unworthy of serious consideration.

But, in fact, there is no best system. In choosing how elections are to be run, officials in every country make decisions that involve trade-offs. It is worth looking at those trade-offs and asking what the implications are of using one set of rules or another. Electoral rules are expressions of priorities in a system of governance. They influence political participation by determining how easy or difficult it is to vote or to be a candidate. Importantly, electoral rules affect how faithfully the elected officeholders reflect society and, in doing so, how they affect officeholding by minority populations and the expression of views and policy preferences often overlooked by powerful groups. Both considerations, access and representation, can affect the peace in and stability of a society. Electoral rules also have impacts on other institutions, such as the fate of smaller parties, the nature of the political party system, and the formation and durability of governments.

Different electoral systems facilitate or limit the emergence and success of new parties, foster either two-party or multiparty systems, and affect the ability of those elected to office to form a government. The more proportional the outcome of an election is, the more likely governance will feature multiple parties and coalition governments. The representational value of proportionality, which is tempered by the complexity that those elected in such a system face in governing, is in contrast to the relative ease of governing that occurs in systems that force electoral majorities at the expense of proportional representation (PR). To return to the examples of Belgium and Israel, both have electoral systems based on proportionality, leading to numerous political parties and often complicated and lengthy negotiations after elections to form a government. The resulting multiparty governments can often be unstable. In contrast, in the United States, electoral rules favor two political parties at the expense of smaller ones. After legislative elections, one party holds a majority

3

WHAT IF THE UNITED STATES HAD A PARLIAMENT?

PREDICTED PARLIAMENT*   TOTAL SEATS **435**

113	124	37	49	112
LEFT	CENTRE-LEFT	CENTRE-RIGHT	RIGHT	POPULIST
"Social Democratic Party"	"Liberal Party"	"Conservative Party"	"Christian Coalition"	"People's Party"
BERNIE SANDERS 26% of vote	HILLARY CLINTON 28%	JOHN KASICH 8%	TED CRUZ 11%	DONALD TRUMP 26%

Sources: YouGov; CPS; *The Economist*   *based on April 22-26th 2016 polling; seats allocated   The Economist
Pic credits: AP; AFP; Getty Images; Reuters   proportionally by census region (North, Midwest, South, West)

1. This graphic shows the 2016 election result in the United States had there been proportionality and multiple parties. If there had been proportionality and multiple parties then, the Social Democratic Party and the Liberal Party would have been able to form a majority— according to public opinion polls. Instead of Donald Trump winning the presidency in a winner-take-all electoral system, the top executive office would likely have gone to Hillary Clinton, as the leader of the largest party.

in the House of Representatives, usually leading to stable governance. The overall result, though, is far from proportional. To illustrate, the *Economist* provided a visual of what the 2016 election result would have been under proportionality with multiple parties vying for seats (based on polling data). A coalition of center-left parties, likely led by Hillary Clinton, would have resulted, rather than a Republican-led government under Donald Trump.

Electoral rules are shaped by historical experience and, typically, by the preferences of system designers when it comes to accessibility to participation in the politics of the system, societal representation, and models of governance. The designers, we can assume, intended to preserve their own electoral advantages. The oldest and simplest modern electoral system, the plurality system, is found in the United Kingdom and many of its former colonies.

In the plurality system, often called first-past-the-post (FPTP), the candidate with the largest share of the vote wins the office or seat. Electoral systems adopted more recently tend to feature PR—where the share of seats a party is awarded is proportionate to its share of the overall vote—or they are hybrids, with some seats won by plurality and some by proportionality. Other countries use preferential voting (PV) systems, allowing voters to rank candidates when casting their ballots. There are many other elements of electoral system design that have consequences for elections and governance. The preferences of the original designers of an electoral system—most often those in power at the time the electoral rules were adopted—determined the system in play, reflecting their political values and benefiting their own power perspectives.

Election systems and their trade-offs matter because they have clear implications for a number of outcomes, including system legitimacy. As an obvious example, the US citizens who protested the results of the 2020 presidential election on January 6, 2021, attempting to prevent the US Congress from certifying the election of Joe Biden, did not believe that he was a legitimate winner. Their skepticism was the result of the ways they perceived the election had been unfair. Because of some aspects of how elections are run in the United States—for example, the roles of local officials in deciding how votes are cast (in person, by mail, dropped at unattended boxes, etc.) and in counting the votes and certifying the winner—those who protested did not think the election had been free and fair.

Similarly, participation in politics is affected by the rules of the system, including who can run for office, who can vote, and how easily citizens can do either. How satisfied are citizens with their system's openness and transparency? If they are dissatisfied, do they understand why, and what alternatives exist? Satisfaction with the process might vary with whether citizens feel they have a fair chance to be represented or elected. Electoral rules impact the chances that women or members of a country's ethnic, racial, or religious minority groups have of becoming candidates or winning office, and that a range of views and experiences will be expressed in government (often through minor political parties). And these all, in turn, have clear implications for a country's ability to manage conflict of all sorts.

If officials understand the implications of trade-offs as they determine electoral rules, the system chosen may well be better suited for the country involved. And if voters understand the system and find its features to be commensurate with the values and principles they hold dear, they may be more likely to approve of the electoral system, and to show that approval by participating in elections and recognizing the legitimacy of election outcomes.

Elections to what?

Electoral rules are one of many institutional features in democratic systems. Electoral rules may be among the easiest political institutions to alter, since changes to them do not necessarily require constitutional amendment; in many cases they are changed through legislation or even administrative actions. The United States is an exception, but not the norm, in that change to some of the fundamental dimensions of the electoral system would require a constitutional amendment. Electoral systems and rules, which determine how elections are run and results determined, interact with other features of political systems, such as the way the government is structured—for example, whether it is presidential or parliamentary, or a hybrid of the two. Many combinations are possible, and some patterns are possible to identify.

Presidential systems feature elections for the top political office, the presidency, where voters cast a vote for a single candidate and the top vote-getter wins the office or seat. In some countries a majority is needed to win, whereas in others, a plurality suffices.

In some countries, like the United States (or the Vatican), votes cast by electors in a body specifically constituted to carry out the election, known as the Electoral College in the United States, determine the winner of the presidency, but in most countries, presidents are chosen by popular vote.

Moreover, when presidential systems elect their legislatures, there may be a range of electoral rules. In the United States, members of the legislature are elected much like the president, minus the Electoral College: voters cast a vote for a candidate in an electoral constituency or district, and the plurality winner of the vote takes the legislative seat. In other presidential systems, however, when electing representatives to the national legislature, voters may cast a vote for a single candidate in their district, or for a political party list, or for both. In Argentina's presidential system, the legislature is elected by PR. In the presidential systems of Mexico, Korea, and Madagascar, the legislatures are elected using FPTP for some seats and PR for others.

Parliamentary systems differ in that voters choose representatives to the legislature, and then the newly elected representatives in the majority party (or coalition of parties) in the legislature choose the prime minister and approve cabinet members. There are two broad types of parliamentary systems, distinguished by their electoral systems and patterns of governance. In the "Westminster" system of the United Kingdom, voters cast a ballot for their member of the House of Commons, and voting is in single-member districts where only one candidate will represent the district—the candidate with a plurality of votes. Once voters have elected members of the Commons, the MPs (Members of Parliament) in the party with the most seats select the prime minister. Typically, citizens vote for their MP based on which party they want to control the government and on whom they prefer as prime minister. Often critical issues separate the parties. Thus, when citizens in the United Kingdom went to the polls in December 2019, they were evaluating Prime Minister Boris

Johnson's leadership, particularly his role in implementing the British withdrawal from the European Union. Johnson's party won a landslide majority of 365 seats out of the total 650 seats, with their closest rival, the Labour Party, gaining only 202 seats; as a result, in the ensuing sessions of Parliament, Johnson was able to implement his Conservative Party's agenda with little effective opposition.

In the United Kingdom, two parties—Conservative and Labour—dominate, though other parties run candidates and win some seats in Parliament. Because of the dominance of the two parties, after most elections one party achieves a majority and forms the government; that party is then able to govern according to its agenda. The UK is a particular type of parliamentary system, a majoritarian one, in large part because of its electoral rules.

Other parliamentary systems have elections in which votes are cast for parties, multiple parties contend for power, and a single party is less likely to win a majority. Most parliaments are not in fact majoritarian but rather are "consensus models," featuring proportional electoral rules, multiple parties, and coalition governments.

And then there are some parliamentary systems that combine plurality rules and proportional representation to elect their legislatures. Some countries even have different electoral systems for the two houses of their legislature. In bicameral Australia, for example, FPTP is used for the House of Representatives and PR for the Senate. In unicameral New Zealand, to illustrate another variation, 72 members of the 120-seat legislature are elected using the majoritarian system and 48 members are chosen based on the political parties' shares of the national vote. The point here is that the type of democratic government, whether presidential or parliamentary, does not dictate the electoral system of the legislature. Likewise, some presidential systems (e.g., the United States) elect their legislatures using candidate-based, plurality methods, while others (e.g., Mexico, Korea, and Madagascar) combine that method with party-focused proportional rules. Still other presidential systems use PR for all seats in their legislatures.

What about the state form—whether a country is federal or unitary, whether the national government is made up of units like states with some of their own power, or whether all power is focused in the national government? Like the form of government and electoral rules, various combinations are possible. Some federal systems, like those of India, Canada, and the United States, have plurality/majoritarian election rules; others, such as Belgium and Austria, have proportional, party-focused elections. Federal Germany combines the two electoral systems.

Federal systems essentially guarantee representation for geographic regions, which in the United States and Australia (and elsewhere) lead some regions to have more legislative seats than their population alone would determine. For example, the US Senate is composed of two members from each of the 50 states, so that tiny Wyoming, with a population of half a million, and California, with 39 million, each has two senators. Many countries also mandate electoral representation for various groups within their population—women, Indigenous people, or citizens living outside of the country's geographic boundaries. Some federal systems, like that of the United States, encompass a variety of electoral rules across their federal states, while others, like Germany, have more uniform rules across the subnational units. The form of government (presidential or parliamentary) and the type of state (unitary or federal) do not dictate the electoral system, but the electoral system influences the nature of competition and governance in every case.

Voting

Electoral systems are a central component of the institutional architecture of a democratic country and have consequences for how well a democracy functions. In addition to their implications for other institutions, such as parties, party systems, and governments, electoral systems also matter a great deal for how political contests are viewed and fought and the nature of public policy. For example, countries vary in terms of how much trust their citizens have that those in charge govern with the best interests of the citizens in mind. One measure of trust in government is whether or not citizens choose to participate through voting. The following table shows turnout in recent elections in a sample of countries. In part, turnout is determined by voting laws. Voting is mandatory, for example, for some elections in more than 25 countries, including Australia and (for some cantons) Switzerland; these polities have various types of sanctions for not voting, and they also vary as to whether these sanctions are effectively imposed.

Among those countries that do not require citizens to vote, there is considerable variation in turnout. What does low turnout reflect in these nations? Perhaps dissatisfaction with the system, or a feeling that it does not matter whether one votes or not, as the outcome in terms of policy will be the same. Or one could argue that low turnout reflects the opposite view, that people are satisfied with those who govern them and feel they will be satisfied no matter who wins. If that is the case, why should they take the time to vote as opposed to spending their time on other activities? What turnout variation reflects and how much trust citizens have in their government might well depend on which citizens one is considering; that is, some citizens might trust the government and vote because of that, while others might not.

Elections determine who will represent citizens in their government. If the electorate does not reflect the population—in terms of turnout or influence—those not represented are more likely to be dissatisfied. Electoral systems vary in terms of how well those with minority views or minority status in a society are represented in elected office. At certain times in history these

Table 1. Turnout among eligible voters in a sample of countries

Region	Country	Percentage of voting age population that voted
North America	Canada	55.43 (2021)
	United States	62.36 (2020)
	Mexico	65.62 (2018)
Central America	Costa Rica	59.79 (2018)
South America	Colombia	52.17 (2018)
	Chile	50.43 (2021)
	Brazil	76.66 (2018)
Europe	United Kingdom	62.04 (2019)
	Ireland	56.65 (2020)
	France	67.93 (2017)
	Germany	69.48 (2021)
	Sweden	82.08 (2018)
	Estonia	56.45 (2019)
Middle East	Israel	73.65 (2021)
Africa	Nigeria	24.86 (2019)
	Ghana	79.99 (2020)
	Kenya	59.77 (2017)
	South Africa	47.28 (2019)
Asia	India	68.80 (2019)
	Japan	55.75 (2021)
	Indonesia	73.03 (2019)
Oceania	Australia	80.79 (2019)
	New Zealand	77.35 (2020)

Source: International Institute for Democracy and Electoral Assistance (International IDEA), www.idea.int/data-tools/country-view/68/40

factors are clear. The movements for women suffrage or racial minority suffrage in various countries at various times have acknowledged evident flaws in earlier representational systems. Finally, electoral systems determine how citizen preferences and citizen votes are converted into governmental policies.

Elections where?

In most countries, elections are held for offices at multiple levels—local, regional, national, and even supranational (e.g., the European Union). Our subject is elections that occur nationally for legislatures and for directly elected heads of state, known in most countries as executive presidents or simply presidents. National elections are the most comparable across countries, and the impacts of electoral rules on these elections are similarly subject to comparison.

The question of which countries' elections we examine requires a bit more clarification. Elections occur in almost every country, but we are concerned only with elections in which competition exists. In some countries, such as Russia or China, elections are regularly held, but the results are generally known in advance. In such countries, one party controls the mechanisms of elections; while the ruling party may tolerate some opposition, no true competition exists. In democracies, to the contrary, elections feature true competition, with candidates competing for support from the electorate and for the right to govern in their name. But even in these countries the amount of competition varies, and how elections are run can differ significantly. In some democracies, one party dominates; in others, more than one party has a legitimate chance for success. The distinguishing factor is that the electoral rules do not preclude criticism of those in power or even a legitimate opportunity to replace incumbent officials with their opponents. How free opponents are to wage campaigns varies from democracy to democracy.

There are various ways to define democracy and distinguish among types of political systems. The V-Dem (Varieties of Democracy) Institute, based at the Department of Political Science at the University of Gothenburg, Sweden categorizes countries as liberal democracies, electoral democracies, electoral autocracies, or closed autocracies. The categorization is based on the evaluation of 40 indicators that specify how elections are run in terms of suffrage, elected officials, clean elections, freedom of association, and freedom of expression, as evaluated by at least five independent evaluators in more than 200 countries. As of March 2022, the V-Dem project categorized 34 countries as liberal democracies, 55 as electoral democracies, 60 as electoral autocracies, and 30 as closed democracies, with recent trends moving in the autocratic direction. The table here lists examples of countries that fit into each of these categories.

Examining competitive elections in some of the 89 nations in V-Dem's two most democratic categories reveals distinctions among the functioning of elections in those systems and the implications of those distinctions for the administration of elections, voter participation, representation, government stability, and other outcomes. In each case, lawmakers have considered or are considering trade-offs as they weigh one set of rules against another. Where appropriate, we examine efforts to reform a nation's (and, where pertinent, a subnational entity's) system, exploring the impetus for reform and the effects of those reforms that were implemented.

Elections function differently in the 89 countries that the V-Dem project deemed to be liberal or electoral democracies. They differ according to who can vote, how the votes are cast, and how they are tabulated. They differ according to which offices are contested (and what powers accrue to those offices). They differ according to how many representatives are elected

Table 2. Examples of countries in each of V-Dem's four categories of countries

Liberal democracies	Electoral democracies	Electoral autocracies	Closed autocracies
Belgium	Argentina	Belarus	China
Canada	Brazil	Cambodia	Cuba
Costa Rica	Czech Republic	Congo	Jordan
Estonia	Georgia	Ethiopia	Libya
Germany	Indonesia	Hungary	North Korea
Ireland	Kosovo	India	Saudi Arabia
Israel	Mexico	Palestine/West Bank	Sudan
Taiwan	Nigeria	The Philippines	Thailand
United Kingdom	Peru	Russia	United Arab Emirates
United States	Poland	Zambia	Vietnam

from each district. They differ in a host of other ways as well, such as how candidates attain the ballot, how they campaign for office, how many parties are on the ballot and how many have real chances of attaining power, how and by whom campaigns are funded, and when and how information about candidates is disseminated to the electorate.

We draw upon examples from a variety of countries' elections, but disproportionately from the American case, for two reasons. Because of controversies in recent elections, US elections are likely to be more familiar than those in other nations. In addition, the United States is a case in which the electoral rules were established some time ago, in the eighteenth century; and, while some would argue they have stood the test of time, others find reasons to look more critically and comparatively at the arrangements, asking whether a system designed more than two centuries ago to answer the needs of that generation of political leaders is appropriate for the twenty-first century. What can be learned from some of the recent elections in the United States? Are there ways of administering elections and translating votes into seats that might improve the functioning of American government and strengthen public trust?

Chapter 2
Electoral systems

The choice of an electoral system says a great deal about a country, its past, and its priorities; it is not just an arbitrary set of rules. An electoral system reflects the designers' self-interest in many ways, such as whether they want to encourage or discourage widespread popular participation in governing, whether they seek to facilitate or to limit the emergence and influence of new parties, or whether they seek a government that reflects regional interests or favors national concerns. The choice of precise rules and features indicates the extent to which designers of electoral systems prioritize the participation of various minority groups in elected offices and wish to see elected bodies reflect the societies that elect them, or whether they prefer to continue the power of dominant elements of the polity.

The role of history is highly relevant for a discussion of electoral rules. Historical ties between countries, namely those stemming from empires and colonialism, may reproduce colonial electoral models in postcolonial settings. The opposite is also true: the legacies of colonialism may lead to a deliberate move away from the systems that appear to be imposed or ill-fitting for current realities. The differing influence of a similar history can be seen in the contrast between the development of the Canadian electoral system, which is clearly patterned on that of the United Kingdom, and that of the Republic of Ireland, which moved away from the FPTP Westminster model in the system Ireland established in 1922.

Some of the oldest democratic political systems feature the simplest rules: in Britain and the United States, for instance, whoever wins the most votes wins the seat or office. Newer systems tend to feature more complex rules designed to remedy perceived weaknesses of older systems, such as the perception that votes cast for losing candidates are "wasted votes," or to produce a desired outcome, such as greater representation of women or other minorities in elected offices and legislative bodies. Men tend to be the beneficiaries of the simplest "winner-take-all" systems. Electoral reforms, such as those in Italy in 2005, typically increase the percentage of women in parliament—which it did in Italy, by 5 percent. Some of the most recent changes to electoral systems feature combinations of systems—reforms meant to achieve twin goals of simplicity and representation.

Electoral systems, then, do not exist in a vacuum. They are usually influenced by models of countries close to them, either geographically, historically, or culturally. Electoral systems are also shaped by other governmental institutions, such as whether a political system is presidential or parliamentary, or whether it is federal or unitary, though neither of these dichotomies leads definitively to any one electoral system. Electoral rules, in turn, have impacts on other institutions, such as political parties and party systems. Moreover, electoral systems are products of their times, which determine the available models as well as the concerns and debates that influence electoral system choices. As officials make decisions regarding how elections are to be run, they are making choices, engaging in trade-offs between the advantages of one system and those of another—for example, between the simplicity in governing implied in majority rule and the complexity of proportional representation of competing ideas, or between the desire to ease access to the ballot for all citizens and the need for security of the ballot that requires some safeguards.

First-time voters may feel a thrill about exercising their most fundamental political right. They may focus on the major issues and personalities in the election campaign, and they may inform themselves on where and when to go to the polls. Beyond that, do they think much about the features of the electoral system and how those features matter? They should, because they do. Electoral systems vary on three fundamental dimensions: the rule for allocating seats in the assembly, that is, for translating votes into election outcomes; the district magnitude, or number of representatives elected from each electoral district; and the number of votes each voter casts, or the ballot structure. (While "district" is the term most often used in the literature on electoral systems, the terms "electorates," "constituencies," "ridings," and simply "seats" are commonly used to mean the same thing in various countries.)

Elections of legislatures

One way to examine electoral systems for legislative elections is to consider their votes-to-seats relationship, and to what extent they produce "wasted" votes (i.e., votes for parties that did not win seats). Low proportionality of votes-to-seats and high wasted votes are generally believed to discourage voting for smaller parties, and perhaps voting at all. With this in mind, it is useful to look more closely at the three main categories of electoral systems: plurality/majority systems, proportional representation (PR) systems, and mixed systems, with variations within each category.

In plurality/majority systems, typically, only one seat is elected per district. In other words, these systems are characterized by geographically defined, single-member districts (SMDs).

Plurality electoral systems, often known as first-past-the-post (FPTP), permit each voter to cast one vote for a single candidate, with the top vote-getter winning the single seat from the district, regardless of whether that candidate has won a majority of the votes cast. This is the simplest system, since there is one round of voting. It is used for parliamentary elections in the United Kingdom and in many, but not all, countries with historical ties to Great Britain.

About a quarter of the lower houses or first chambers of legislatures throughout the world are elected using FPTP.

Some systems require that a candidate win an absolute majority of the vote. There are two ways that can happen. In the two-round system (TRS), used in fewer than 10 percent of the countries, if no candidate wins an absolute majority of the votes cast, a second round of voting takes place at a later date. Typically, only the top two candidates, or only those who have won a certain percentage of the vote, can proceed to the second round of voting. For example, in French parliamentary elections, when no candidate wins a majority in the first vote, candidates who have won 12.5 percent of the registered electorate in their district advance to the runoff. To win the seat, a candidate need only win the plurality in the second round. The TRS is used by 22 legislatures worldwide, mostly in countries with historical links to France. This system tends to promote bargaining among parties and candidates between the first and second rounds. Candidates who do not advance to a runoff, and their supporters, have another chance to influence the result, making their support valuable to candidates in the runoff.

In preferential voting (PV), used in legislative elections in just a few countries (Australia, Papua New Guinea, and, until 2013, Fiji), voters can make their preferences for candidates known by ranking candidates when they cast their vote. Also known as alternative voting (AV), ranked choice voting, or instant runoff voting, under these rules, if a candidate wins the absolute majority of first preferences/rankings, that candidate is elected. If no candidate wins an absolute majority, the candidate with the lowest number of first preferences is eliminated and the ballots cast for the candidate are transferred to their second preferences; if that produces a majority winner, that candidate receives the seat. If there still is no majority winner, the process continues, eliminating the next lowest vote-getters, and transferring their votes, until a majority is won by one candidate. Proponents of PV point out that it leads to a centrist, cooperative style of politics, since it encourages candidates to seek to appeal to a wider audience, not simply their core voters, as they may need the supporters of other candidates to win a majority. This voting system also has the advantage of producing a winner who has received majority support, even if as second or third choice, as opposed to one who has only plurality support and may be strongly opposed by all other voters.

Unless a small party has supporters concentrated in specific districts, it is unlikely to win seats in plurality/majority systems. The largest parties, typically the largest two, are favored in these systems. Advantages of this type of electoral system include its simplicity for voters and for calculating winners—a single candidate for a single seat from a geographically defined district.

Plurality systems typically result in effective governance, since small parties are usually kept out of assemblies or win a small number of seats, allowing a larger party to form a single-party government that will be likely to pass its agenda and last the full legislative term. In addition, since only one representative is sent to the legislature from each district, that person stands as a visible link between the governing system and the electorate. Voters know whom to credit or blame for policy successes and failures. Elected representatives are beholden to voters in their districts rather than to their political party.

But there are also downsides to this simplest electoral model: since only one person is elected from a district, all of those who voted for candidates who lost may see their votes as wasted, which can, in turn, affect perceptions of the winner as a legitimate representative of those who did not vote for that candidate. This perception is particularly true of systems that do not require a majority winner; it could produce a situation where a majority of the voters may consider their votes wasted, and thus may feel that elected institutions do not legitimately represent them. Those whose candidates always lose in a certain district may feel that voting is fruitless and not turn out at all. In the United States, Republican turnout is low in heavily Democratic Massachusetts, while Democratic turnout is low in Republican-dominated Oklahoma. These all have negative consequences for citizen perception of the legitimacy of government.

This system also tends to reward larger parties and give them a manufactured majority. The effect is to discourage the emergence of new parties—or at least new parties with national support—and to prevent small parties that represent minority interests from gaining office. Consider the discrepancy between the share of the vote won and the share of seats won by the Conservative Party in the general elections in the UK from 2010 to 2019:

Table 3. Share of the vote and of the seats in the UK House of Commons won by the Conservative Party

Year	Percentage of vote share	Percentage of seat share
2010	36.1	47.1
2015	36.8	50.8
2017	42.3	48.8
2019	43.6	56.2

In none of those four elections did the Conservatives come close to winning a majority of the votes across the country, yet the party "won" every election, allowing it to lead the government in each case. In 2010, the Conservatives, led by David Cameron, formed a coalition—a rarity in the UK, where single-party governments are the norm—with the Liberal Democrats. In 2015, the Conservatives won only 36.8 percent of the national vote, but it squeaked out victories in a majority of the districts, giving it a total of 50.8 percent of the seats in Parliament, allowing Cameron to lead a single-party government. While 50.8 percent is a very small majority, the point is that in 2015 there was a huge discrepancy between the party's national share of the vote and the seats it was awarded in the legislature. In 2017, the discrepancy between the Conservatives' share of the national vote, 42.3 percent, and its share of seats, 48.8 percent, was much less. Still, the party lacked a majority needed to lead a government, so it formed a minority government—also a rarity in the UK—with agreement from the small Northern Irish Democratic Unionist Party (DUP) to support the Conservatives' legislative agenda. In 2019, the Conservatives won about the same percentage of the national vote as in the previous election in 2017, with 43.6 percent, but it was the winner-that-took-all in more than a majority of the district contests, giving it 56.2 percent of the seats. For small parties like the Liberal Democrats, electoral distortion typically works in the opposite direction; in the 2010 election, for example, the party won 23 percent of the vote nationally, but to win seats, it must win the most votes in SMDs. When the votes were tallied in each district, it was awarded only 8.8 percent of the seats in Parliament. In other electoral systems, its share of seats would be much more likely to approximate its share of votes.

Proportional representation (PR) is the most common electoral system in democracies, and it is the dominant system in Latin America, Europe, and Africa. It is often forgotten that in the early part of the twentieth century, many cities in the United States experimented with PR electoral rules, with positive effects for the proportionality of election outcomes. Most cities abandoned PR for plurality rules, however, due largely to complaints of politicians and parties who lost influence, and of those who feared the gains in representation made by minorities.

Proponents of PR highlight its potential for including a range of groups in polities with socially divided populations and for helping promote trust after periods of conflict. The idea underpinning this type of electoral system is that a party's share of the national vote will as faithfully as possible be mirrored in the legislature. That is, if a party wins 20 percent of the national vote, it will receive 20 percent of the seats in the chamber. All PR systems have multimember districts (MMDs), which means more than one person represents the district in parliament. The higher the number of seats elected from a district—the district magnitude—the more closely the legislators elected will proportionally reflect the electorate's vote. Some countries, like Israel and the Netherlands, are a single electoral district with district magnitude equal to the size of the legislature (120 and 150 seats, respectively); the legislators elected in those countries reflect the voters' preferences quite accurately, though many small parties represented in the legislature might make it more difficult to form a majority government following an election.

The most common form of PR is the party-list PR system, in which each party composes a list of candidates, and voters cast a vote for one party list. Each party is awarded the number of seats that is proportional to its share of the vote. So if a party wins 10 percent of the vote, it gets 10 percent of the seats. How do the parties know which candidates get to take the seats? A party's seats are filled by candidates based on the order in which they appear on the party list. To give a concrete example, in 2021 in the Netherlands, Mark Rutte's People's Party for Freedom and Democracy (VVD) won 22 percent of the national vote, giving his party 34 seats in the 120-seat parliament. The rest of the candidates, numbers 35 and beyond on the VVD's party list, were not seated. For each of the other Dutch parties, the same process occurs: national votes for a party list determine the number of seats a party is awarded, which determines the number of candidates taken off the top of a party's list.

PR list systems can employ either closed or open party lists. In closed list systems, such as in Spain and Portugal, party leaders decide the order of the candidates on their lists, and voters cannot change that order. In closed list systems, candidates are beholden to party leaders for inclusion on the list at all, and for their precise placement on the list; the higher they are on the list, the greater the chances of gaining a seat in the legislature. Therefore, closed list systems usually feature campaigning styles that focus on the party program. In open list systems, as in Brazil and Sri Lanka, voters may change the order of names on the party list of their choice. In that case, candidates are less beholden to the party, resulting in a campaign style that focuses more on appealing to voters and, once elected, greater focus on constituents than might be the case in a closed list system. For those reasons, open lists may be seen as having more democratic legitimacy.

List PR systems may have electoral thresholds that parties must reach in order to win seats in the legislature; for example, a threshold of 5 percent means that parties polling less than 5 percent do not receive any seats in the legislature. The thresholds affect the overall proportionality of the system. High thresholds will present barriers for the smallest parties, leading to fewer parties represented in the legislature and reducing proportionality of the system. If a threshold is high, voters for parties that do not surpass it may feel that their votes are wasted. Where there is no threshold or a very low one, in contrast, smaller parties will have a greater chance of representation and the overall result will be highly proportional. In the Netherlands, for example, there is no electoral threshold, so parties can win a seat in the parliament with about 70,000 votes. In 2021, 17 parties won seats. The coalition government that formed after the election had four parties. Had there been a 5 percent electoral threshold, only 8 parties would have won seats. The votes for the 9 parties that did not surpass the threshold would have been "wasted," although they would have been redistributed among the 8 that did, proportionate to their share of the vote. The outcome for post-election government coalition-building in that case might have been simpler, resulting in fewer parties in the cabinet.

PR systems have several advantages. First, for voters, there is a greater likelihood that their vote will be cast for a party that has a chance of being elected in MMDs, especially if the district magnitude is relatively high and the threshold for entering the legislature is relatively low. Thus, PR systems have fewer "wasted votes" than plurality and majority systems; as a result, we might expect turnout to be higher. Second, bodies elected by PR tend to be more representative of the society and its divisions—ideological or policy divisions, or demographic divisions—and, as a consequence, are accessible to smaller parties and more inclusive of minorities. With the importance of party lists in PR systems, candidates and parties are encouraged to appeal to voters across the country rather than cater to particular regions or constituencies.

Critics cite some disadvantages of PR. In particular, the fragmentation of the vote across numerous parties makes single-party (and thus simpler) government less likely and coalition governments more common. Though coalition governments are seen by some as beneficial to divided or postconflict societies, others note that they can slow down the legislative process and even lead to gridlock. Critics point out that the lower barrier for entry (especially in countries with low electoral thresholds) also makes it easier for extremist parties to gain seats in a legislature. The point is that there are trade-offs.

There is another MMD system, the single transferable vote (STV) system, used only in the direct elections to lower houses in the Republic of Ireland and in Malta (and for local elections in other countries). Voters may rank as many or as few candidates as they like, but they must designate at least their first preference. This system uses a quota for election from the district. (The quota is the total number of votes in the election divided by the number of seats in a district, plus 1. To that number, a 1 is added. For example, if 500 votes are cast in an MMD with 4 seats, the quota would be 101.) Once votes are counted, any candidates meeting or surpassing the quota are elected. Their surplus votes are then redistributed according to second preferences. The votes are again counted and any candidates now meeting the quota are elected. If none meet the quota, the candidate with the lowest vote count is eliminated and his or her votes are redistributed according to second preferences. This continues until all of the seats in the MMD are filled. The outcome is fairly proportional. Since voters are ranking candidates rather than voting for parties, this system makes it easier for independent candidates to be elected.

Mixed systems combine plurality/majority and PR systems in an effort to produce the best of both worlds: providing a direct connection between voters and their representatives while also producing a chamber that is proportional in its representation of voters and their preferences. Most mixed systems do this in a parallel way, meaning the seats elected on the basis of PR in MMDs are not linked to the seats elected by plurality in SMDs. Voters in these systems, called mixed-member majoritarian (MMM), cast two votes, one for a party and one for a candidate in their electoral district. The proportion of seats elected by PR and non-PR methods varies across countries, as does the non-PR method used to elect legislators from SMDs. As the table below shows, Japan elects 37.5 percent of its parliamentary seats with PR and 62.5 percent of the seats in SMDs using FPTP, winner-take-all system. Lithuania's parliament is split 50-50. In both cases, the outcome of elections in the SMDs does not affect the outcome of the PR election in the MMDs held at the same time. An advantage of these models is the relative simplicity of administering these elections.

In mixed-member proportional (MMP) systems, which account for far fewer national legislative elections, the PR and non-PR votes are linked to determine the overall result. For the non-PR vote, most of the countries use FPTP balloting, and only Hungary uses a TRS. Like parallel mixed systems, linked systems have a range of ratios of PR to non-PR seats. In contrast to parallel mixed systems, however, when the votes are tallied in MMP systems, if the plurality/majority vote for a party falls short of the share it would be permitted under the PR vote, the difference between the two votes is the number of candidates the party may take from its list to send to parliament. In that instance, the PR lists are used to "top-up" and compensate for the disproportionality of the plurality/majority vote. For example, in Germany's 2021 election, the Greens won 14.8 percent of the national vote, entitling them to 85 seats. The party also won 16 of the SMD contests. Subtracting the "direct mandates" from the SMDs (16) from the total number of seats (85) would allow the Greens to take 69 candidates off their party list. (In reality, Germany's system is much more complex than that; party lists are drawn up in each of the 16 federal states, plus there are rules that award parties additional seats.) The following table shows the two types of mixed systems, parallel (MMM) and linked (MMP), and notes the variation within each type.

Table 4. Share of seats elected by proportional representation (PR) and non-PR methods in selected countries (FPTP is first-past-the-post, or plurality; TRS is two-round system, which ensures a majority; PR is proportional representation)

a. Parallel elections (MMM)

Country	Percentage of PR seats	Percentage of Non-PR seats	Non-PR system
Armenia	43	57	FPTP
Azerbaijan	20	80	TRS
Guinea	67	33	FPTP
Japan	37.5	62.5	FPTP
Korea	19	81	FPTP
Lithuania	50	50	TRS
Ukraine	50	50	FPTP

b. Linked elections (MMP)

Country	Percentage of PR seats	Percentage of Non-PR seats	Non-PR system
Albania	29	71	FPTP
Bolivia	48	52	FPTP
Germany	50	50	FPTP
Hungary	54	46	TRS
Mexico	40	60	FPTP
New Zealand	46	56	FPTP

Why have all these different systems emerged? What were their designers thinking? In each case, those writing the rules understood how small changes could lead to different results. That is why the rules are so important. One can deduce the political goal of the system designer from the system and the rules within the system they chose. The MMP system in Germany tries to achieve an overall result that is proportional—where numbers of seats reflect electoral strength—but its designers did not want to give up the direct link between voters and their representatives. However, the system is complex, both in terms of voters' understanding of how votes are translated into seats and in terms of the administration of the elections. Another downside might be in creating two categories of legislators: those elected by FPTP with a strong link to voters and those elected by PR who are more beholden to their parties.

Another important decision that designers of electoral systems must consider is the number of representatives or legislative seats to be elected in each legislative district. FPTP, PV, and TRS systems elect only one representative per district, so they obviously have a district magnitude of one. In elections featuring PR, legislative districts will be multimember, meaning more than one person will be elected to office. The higher the district magnitude, or the number of legislators elected in a district, the more proportional the vote-to-seat ratio will be. The downsides of such systems are the relatively weak linkage between voters and their representatives and the relative ease with which extremist parties' candidates can be elected to the legislature. The more fragmented the vote and more multiparty the legislature, the harder it may be to form coalition governments in parliamentary systems or to pass legislation in a timely manner. Furthermore, coalition governments composed of several parties, sometimes including very small parties, may be unstable. District magnitudes at the extreme low or high ends could be problematic—if too low, small parties are disadvantaged and representation is not very proportional, but if they are too high, the number of parties entering the legislature is likely to increase, making governing more difficult.

"Ballot structure" is a feature of all electoral systems that draws our attention to what the voters actually see on Election Day and how they cast their vote. In a plurality/majority system, voters have one choice among several candidates.

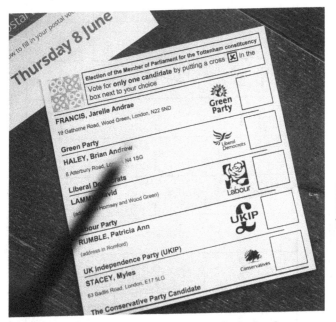

2. **Voters in Britain's plurality electoral system check a box for one candidate, and the highest vote-getter wins. This ballot was for parliamentary elections in 2017.**

In TRSs, the ballot structure refers to what the voter sees as well as the act of holding two separate voting events, where no candidate wins in the first round of voting.

In PR systems, voters may see a ballot that asks them to simply check the party they prefer.

Amtlicher Stimmzettel

für die
Nationalratswahl am 15. Oktober 2017
Regionalwahlkreis 7A - Innsbruck

Liste Nr.	1	2	3	4	5 leer	6	7	8	9	10	11
Partei-bezeichnung	Sozialdemokratische Partei Österreichs	Liste Sebastian Kurz – die neue Volkspartei	Freiheitliche Partei Österreichs	Die Grünen – Die Grüne Alternative		NEOS – Das Neue Österreich und Liberales Forum, gemeinsam mit Irmgard Griss, BürgerInnen und Grünbewegung Verantwortung	Freie Liste Österreich, 4. FPS, Liste Dr. Karl Schnell	Liste Roland Düringer – Meine Stimme GILT	Kommunistische Partei Österreichs und PlattformPlus – offene Liste	Liste Peter Pilz	Die Weissen – Das Recht geht von Volk aus, Wir alle entscheiden in Österreich. Die Volksbewegung
Kurz-bezeichnung	SPÖ	ÖVP	FPÖ	GRÜNE		NEOS	FLÖ	GILT	KPÖ	PILZ	WEIẞE
Für die gewählte Partei ein X einsetzen	○	○	○	○		○	○	○	○	○	○

VORZUGSSTIMME – BUNDESWAHLVORSCHLAG
VORZUGSSTIMME – LANDESWAHLKREIS
VORZUGSSTIMME – REGIONALWAHLKREIS

1	2	3	4		6	7	8	9	10	11
1 MAG. YILDIRIM ○ Selma, 1958	1 THALER ○ Johann, 1962	1 HAAGER ○ Christian, 1948	1 DR. INGRAM ○ Herbert, 1957		1 MAG. ZEDEL ○ Julia, 1991	1 ING. FISCHER ○ Jörg, 1954	1 DÜRINGER ○ Wolfgang, 1975	1 MMAG. STEFFINGER ○ Robert, 1978	1 CHELUCCI ○ Dario, 1976	1 MAG. GARBER ○ Andreas, 1977
2 MIMM ○ Bianca Christian, 1993	2 MAG. FALCH ○ Reinhold, 1966	2 DENISS ○ Julia Anna, 1993	2 MAG. SCHWARZL ○ Lukas, 1988		2 DR. KÖTTINGER ○ Bernhard, 1969	2 Henrij, 1986	2 WELSCH ○ Klaudia Johanna-Sophie, 1966	2 PASZYNIN ○ Doris, 1966	2 HENDLER ○ Brigitte, 1968	
3 SCHAFFER ○ Clemens, 1988	3 KURZ ○ Maximilian, 1985	3 MAG. KLINGLER ○ Tobias Anton, 1983	3 DR. KRAMMER-STÜRN ○ Renate, 1971		3 MAG. KLINGLER ○ Christian Oliver, 1968	3 KÖB ○ Rainer, 1949		3 GINZ ○ Wolfgang, 1958	3 DR. BENGER ○ Josef, 1954	
4 GASSER ○ Stefan Erwin Rudolf, 1992	4 HÖCK ○ Christian, 1985	4 GREGORIN ○ Dietrich, 1969	4 LICHTLEITNER ○ Thomas, 1985		4 LINDENAT ○ Maximilian, 1983	4 PILINGER ○ Edgar, 1959		4 OBERMAIR ○ Christina, 1974	4 GÜTTNER ○ Astrid, 1938	
5 HÖTZL ○ Claudia, 1979	5 GRÜBIC ○ Johann, 1953	5 KUNST ○ Barbara, 1980	5 WEILER ○ Patrick, 1986		5 MAG. PALLHUBER ○ Patrick, 1986	5 PRANTL ○ Heinz, 1951		5 FRITZ ○ Martin, 1952	5 DR. GÖRTLER ○ Werner, 1951	
6 BRENNSTEINER ○ Rudolf, 1969	6 REBIK ○ Markus, 1989	6 HOLAUS ○ Waldemann, 1978	6 DAXNER ○ Sebastian, 1989		6 BALSER ○ Reinhard, 1960	6 ERHART ○ Walter, 1960				
7 ALLABAUER ○ Roman Georg, 1981	7 STAHLER ○ Lorenz, 1983	7 RIECHTHALER ○ Peter, 1980	7 HÖRMANN ○ Angelina, 1992		7 MAG. AIGNE ○ Michael, 1970	7 OSTERWINTHALER ○ Andreas, 1965				
8 RAUCHHÄUSER ○ Helmut Josef, 1957	8 DENZ ○ Astrid, 1957	8 DENZ ○ Astrid, 1957	8 MAG. SCHMID ○ Julia Johanna, 1983		8 NIEDERWIMMER ○ Jakob, 1990					
9 KLEIN ○ Bernhard, 1949	9 MAG. DR. MOSLING ○ Hermann, 1959	9 MAG. DENZ ○ Elmar, 1959	9 MAG. FRITZ ○ Christine, 1958		9 MAG. WINDISCHLER ○ Christian, 1978					
10 HAUSTER ○ Sabine Erika Anna, 1969	10 APPLER ○ Roswitha, 1948	10 DIPL. ING. SCHEICHINGER ○ Evelyn, 1965	10 MAG. HAYS ○ Johann, 1956		10 STEINBERGER ○ Anton, 1973					
11 ...	11 KORLINGER ○ Martin, 1955	11 MAG. JENNEITZEGER ○ Helmut, 1959	11 WELLI ○ Jessica Carina, 1983		11 KOLB ○ Jessica Carina, 1983					
12 PEER ○ Franz Josef, 1958	12 POCK ○ Peter, 1959	12 FENDERSPIEL ○ Rudolf, 1945	12 CHHY ○ Jessica, 1990		12 SCHUMACHER ○ Lukas, 1988					

3. This is a ballot from the 2017 Austrian legislative election, where voters chose a political party rather than an individual candidate.

30

In a mixed electoral system like New Zealand's and Germany's, a voter will see a ballot with two sides, each corresponding to one of the two electoral systems—the List PR vote and the FPTP vote for an individual candidate.

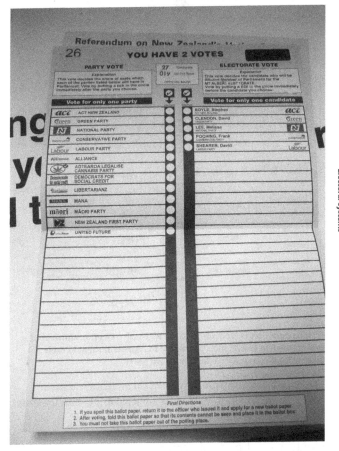

4. In New Zealand, voters cast a first vote for a political party and a second vote for a candidate to represent their district. This ballot was from the 2011 legislative election.

Stimmzettel
für die Wahl zum Deutschen Bundestag
im Wahlkreis 5 Kiel
am 18. September 2005

Sie haben 2 Stimmen

hier 1 Stimme		hier 1 Stimme
für die Wahl eines Wahlkreisabgeordneten	**(X) (X)**	für die Wahl einer Landesliste (Partei) - maßgebende Stimme für die Verteilung der Sitze insgesamt auf die einzelnen Parteien -

Erststimme   Zweitstimme

#	Erststimme		Zweitstimme	#
1	**Dr. Bartels, Hans Peter** Angestellter Kiel Esmarchstraße 16 — SPD — Sozialdemokratische Partei Deutschlands	○	○ **SPD** — Sozialdemokratische Partei Deutschlands — Dr. Ernst Dieter Rossmann, Bettina Hagedorn, Franz Thönnes, Gabriele Hiller-Ohm, Sönke Rix	1
2	**Dr. Murmann, Philipp** Geschäftsführer Heikendorf Hardenbergblick 3 — CDU — Christlich Demokratische Union Deutschlands	○	○ **CDU** — Christlich Demokratische Union Deutschlands — Wolfgang Börnsen, Dr. Ole Schröder, Anke Eymer, Otto Bernhardt, Gero Storjohann	2
3	**Müller, Klaus** Diplom-Volkswirt Kiel Wilhelminenstraße 29 — GRÜNE — BÜNDNIS 90/DIE GRÜNEN	○	○ **GRÜNE** — BÜNDNIS 90/DIE GRÜNEN — Krista Sager, Rainder Steenblock, Monika Heinold, Sebastian David Fricke, Erika von Kalben	3
4	**Blumenthal, Sebastian** Angestellter Kiel Hamburger Chaussee 46 — FDP — Freie Demokratische Partei	○	○ **FDP** — Freie Demokratische Partei — Jürgen Koppelin, Dr. Christel Happach-Kasan, Sebastian Blumenthal, Wolfgang Schnabel, Dr. Michaela Blank	4
5	**Thoroe, Björn** arbeitssuchend Kiel Feldstraße 97 — DIE LINKE. — Die Linkspartei. Schleswig-Holstein	○	○ **DIE LINKE.** — Die Linkspartei. Schleswig-Holstein — Lutz Heilmann, Heidi Beutin, Wiebke Misfeldt, Björn Thoroe, Brigitta Wendt	5
6	**Gutsche, Hermann** EDV-Berater Kiel Königstraße 22 — NPD — Nationaldemokratische Partei Deutschlands	○	○ **NPD** — Nationaldemokratische Partei Deutschlands — Uwe Schäfer, Jens Lütke, Ingo Stawitz, Wolfgang Schimmel, Alfred Hennig	6
7	**Mrozewski, Oliver** Koch Altenholz Danziger Straße 6 — FAMILIE — FAMILIEN-PARTEI DEUTSCHLANDS	○	○ **FAMILIE** — FAMILIEN-PARTEI DEUTSCHLANDS — Matthias Kortলet, Werner Lahann, Sabine Cavid, Hilke Rohlfshagen, Bettina Kortjen	7
8			○ **MLPD** — Marxistisch-Leninistische Partei Deutschlands — Jakobus Fröhlich, Inga Marbach, Andrea Sibylle Hähnel, Joachim Griesbaum, Maria Mayer	8

5. This ballot from Germany's 2005 legislative election shows that voters cast a first vote for a candidate to represent them in their district and a second vote for a political party.

The same ballot structure would pertain in a parallel mixed system, although the way the votes are related, and thus the seats tabulated, would be different.

Elections of heads of state

In parliamentary systems, prime ministers are heads of government and typically chosen by legislatures or by the party or coalition of parties with a majority of the seats won in the legislative election. Heads of state, presidents or chief executives (who are not monarchs), are elected in a variety of ways, depending on history and the interests of system designers.

FPTP/plurality is used to elect presidents directly in more than 20 countries. The advantage of FPTP is that it is inexpensive to operate, easy, and efficient. A disadvantage is that it can produce a winner with less than a majority of the votes, which could undermine public confidence or make it difficult for executives to exercise their authority. A majority outcome is delivered by the TRS system and also the PV system, which allows voters to rank their preferences. PV is used to elect the Irish president.

Where executives are not elected directly, electors representing different organizations or entities elect the president by either plurality in one round, or by a majority, or supermajority, in any number of systems that extend the voting until the required threshold is reached. This system has roots in the Holy Roman Empire, where nobles elected kings. It continues to be used by the Holy See, whereby a College of Cardinals elects the pope through a process often requiring many ballots before the necessary two-thirds supermajority is achieved. Electoral colleges are also used today by countries as different from each other as Estonia, India, Trinidad and Tobago, and the United States.

In the United States, each state chooses a number of electors equal to the number of its representatives in the House of Representatives (thus a number that reflects the population) plus two (each state's number of US senators, reflecting the continuing political power of the states). Electors are chosen by popular vote in each state, with the actual individuals serving as electors chosen by the political parties with the approval of the party's presidential candidate. In all states (and the District of Columbia) other than Maine and Nebraska, whichever candidate polls the most votes in the election receives all of that state's electoral votes. (That provision is determined by state law; Maine and Nebraska divide their electors by congressional district, with the statewide winner receiving two congressional votes, and then one electoral vote to the winner in each electoral district, of which there are two in Maine and three in Nebraska. Reflecting states' prerogatives, Maine's electors within the districts and statewide are chosen using the preferential vote system known as Ranked Choice Voting [RCV] giving minor parties on the presidential ballot some power in a hotly contested race.)

To be elected president in the United States, a candidate must receive a majority of the 538 electoral votes. If no one receives the required 270 votes, the election is decided by the House of Representatives from among the top three vote-getters; in that election, each state is given one vote, determined by a majority vote of its delegation or divided in half if the delegation is split, again reflecting the residual power of the states. Presidential candidates and vice presidential candidates run as one ticket, but in a quirk reflecting historical patterns, should no ticket receive a majority of the electoral votes, while the president is chosen by the House, the vice president is chosen by the Senate; thus, it is theoretically possible for the president and vice president to come from tickets that ran against each other.

Surely no one would design a system like this one today. It was the result of a political compromise between large and small states, between industrial interests and agrarian, slave-holding states. It was adopted before political parties emerged with the full understanding that George Washington, revered by all, would be elected as the first president—and he was, unanimously.

But why does it persist? Recent experiences have shown the disadvantages of the system. Candidates can be elected even though they received, in some cases, far fewer votes than their losing opponents. Because state votes are cast in winner-take-all systems in most American states, there is little incentive to campaign in states a candidate knows will be either lost or won by a large margin; thus, state influence is very uneven, with hotly contested "battleground states" receiving virtually all of the candidates' attention and campaign money. As a result, citizens in many states feel they have no role in the election—their candidate is assured either to win or to lose their state, so why should they vote? The 2020 election even revealed the threat of manipulating the electoral votes after the popular vote has been cast.

The Electoral College system as it functions today is a disaster, but to abolish it, a constitutional amendment is required—and that takes a two-thirds vote in each house of Congress and approval of three-quarters of the states. Small, rural states, some of which feel they benefit from the current system, are overrepresented in the Congress, particularly in the Senate, and thus have the power to halt any amendment. In addition, one party or the other always seems to benefit from the political landscape. Thus, in the climate of the early twenty-first century, it is easier for the Republicans to win under the Electoral College system than it would be under popular vote, so they resist change; at other times, the Democrats thought they had the advantage, and they resisted change. Well short of abolishing the Electoral College, states could, like Maine and Nebraska, change the way their electors are chosen.

When it works correctly, as it has done in the vast majority of elections in its more than 200 years since the Twelfth Amendment linked votes for president and vice president, the system produces a majority winner, a president whose stated majority is often exaggerated, but which adds to the president's ability to govern. Any reform effort in the United States will face intense political headwinds. Since reformers could not move forward after the elections of 2000, 2016, and 2020, optimism about future reform is not high.

To avoid the problem in the United States of electing a candidate to the highest office with a minority of the popular vote, most countries require a candidate to have won a majority (or a large plurality) of the vote in two rounds of voting, if necessary. Some countries require a majority in the first round of voting, and, if no candidate achieves that, typically the two top vote-getters proceed to a runoff (second round) in two weeks or so. The French presidential election of 2022 is an example of this procedure, with the top two vote-getters in the first round, Emmanuel Macron (La Republique En Marche! [LEM]) and Marine Le Pen (Rally Nationale [RN]), facing each other in a runoff election in which Macron expanded his margin over Le Pen to 18 percent, significantly more than the less than 5 percent margin in the first round, in which other candidates together received approximately half of the votes. This "majority-runoff" system is found not only in France but also in Francophone Africa and Latin America.

In Costa Rica, there is a threshold of 40 percent of the votes cast in the first round to win the presidency. Sierra Leone requires 55 percent in the first round. In these cases, if the threshold is not met in first round, there must be a runoff.

Other adaptations of the TRS include distribution requirements, with different thresholds for winning in the first round required in a certain number of subnational units. Such adaptations are found in larger, more heterogeneous countries and typically require that a candidate win an absolute majority of votes cast nationally plus a certain number of votes in a specific number of subnational units. For example, Kenya requires an absolute majority of votes cast plus at least 25 percent of votes in half of Kenya's counties. Similarly, Nigeria requires a majority of votes cast nationally plus at least 25 percent of votes in 24 of 36 states to win the presidency.

Is there a best system?

Electoral systems represent trade-offs between simplicity and accountability, on the one hand, and proportionality and fairness to smaller parties, on the other. While there is no best system, there could be a best system for a particular country. Understanding what that system would be involves a careful discussion of the values to be prioritized in an electoral system. In a country with deep cultural, ethnic, or religious divisions, a system that softens differences might be preferred. In a smaller, more homogeneous system, a majority rule system might be preferable to one emphasizing PR, because such a system makes it easier to govern.

Government leaders know the system in which they have been elected and now govern. It takes truly enlightened leaders to examine the origins of their electoral system, to put aside temporary advantages that happen to favor one party or another at a particular moment in a nation's political life, and to analyze what is best for the country moving forward. Newly formed democracies, such as those that formed after the collapse of communism in Eastern Europe, have an advantage in looking at examples throughout the world and choosing what is best for them. More have chosen parliamentary systems that prioritize PR over presidential systems or others that favor majoritarianism. And occasionally, as happened in Ireland in 1922 or in New Zealand in 1993, leaders find that the moment is right for fundamental examination and reform—and move in that direction, seeking the best system for their country.

Chapter 3
Voting

The act of voting is the means by which citizens make their judgments on those who govern in a democracy. As such, it is fundamental to the effective functioning of a representative democracy. But democratic countries vary significantly in how their citizens vote.

Democratic systems vary on two dimensions. First, countries differ in terms of who is eligible to vote. The norm in the democracies is universal suffrage, but even that concept is more nuanced than one might imagine. How is citizenship defined for the purposes of voting? Can noncitizens, such as those living in a country, applying for citizenship, and on track to be granted citizenship status, vote? Is there a minimum age to define those with the rights of citizenship?

Second, even after the threshold for citizenship has been considered, democracies differ in terms of which citizens are eligible to vote, a concept that distinguishes the voting-age population of a country from the voting-eligible population. Can those convicted of crimes vote? While in jail? After their release? Is there a residency requirement? Where do people who move cast their ballots? Must eligible citizens register to vote, or are they automatically accepted when they turn up at the polls? In some nations the registered voting population is significantly different from the voting-eligible population. And countries differ in terms of how many of those who might vote—under whichever of these definitions one is using—actually turn out to vote, and for which offices.

The choices—who can vote (a choice by a polity), who does vote (individual choices), ease or difficulty in voting (polity choices that affect individual choices)—are important, as they result in significant political and policy consequences. Polities make choices in setting the rules for elections that are trade-offs—between administrative efficiency and ease of voting by citizens, for example—but the consequences of these decisions for the democratic process require closer examination.

Who is eligible to vote?

The norm among democracies is for suffrage to be granted to all citizens. But, of course, that has not always been the case. Although there is some variation, and newer democracies have often granted universal suffrage in their initial constitutions, a historical pattern is clear. First, as kings and other monarchs ceded all or some of their power to the people, suffrage was granted only to property owners. As a working class developed, independent of owning property, nations began granting the right to vote to all males. Women earned suffrage on a country-by-country basis after intense and often extended campaigns in the late nineteenth and early twentieth centuries, or even as late as the mid-twentieth century in countries such as France (1944) and Switzerland (1971). In countries with a history of slavery, emancipation often led to suffrage, though former slaves were frequently excluded from voting through laws that made exercising the franchise difficult. In countries with a direct tie between church and state, those not in the dominant religion were often granted suffrage as part of a democratizing reform. The age of suffrage continues to vary from nation to nation, with the pattern less clear. The following table gives examples of when various groups were enfranchised in a group of democracies.

Elections

Table 5. Attainment of suffrage by various groups in a sample of countries

Region	Country	All men	Women	Racial/ethnic minorities	Minority religion
North America	Canada	1920 (no property exclusions)	1918 (with property) 1920 (all women)	1948 for Asian Canadians, never specific exclusions for Persons of Color	1867 (but there were exclusions during war)
	USA	Left up to states	1920 (19th Amend.)	1870 Black men (15th Amend.) 1925 Native Americans	Left up to states, but in 1965 Voting Rights Act nationally
	Mexico	1917	1953	1917	1917
Central America	Costa Rica	1918	1949		
South America	Colombia	1936	1954	1936	1936
	Chile	1970	1970	1970 (all were limited by ability to read and write until 1970)	1970

(continued)

		1891 (but not illiterates)	Allowed in 1932, compulsory and equal to men in 1945	1891 (no illiterates could vote until 1985)	1891
	Brazil				
Europe	United Kingdom	1918	1928	1791	1791
	Ireland	1923	1923	1791	1791
	France	1848 (except no military)	1944	1792	1848 slavery abolished, but all men voted in election of 1792
	Germany	1871	1918	1919	1919
	Sweden	1909 (25+ to one house of Parliament), 1919 (23+ age)	1919	1873	1838 Jews could vote but not stand for election, Catholics in 1873
	Estonia	1917	1918 (independence from Russia)	1917	1917

Table 5. Continued

Region	Country	All men	Women	Racial/ethnic minorities	Minority religion
Middle East	Israel	1948	1948	1948	1948
Africa	Nigeria		1954 for women in the southern and eastern regions, 1979 for the north		
	Ghana	1951	1951	1951	1951
	Kenya	1923	1923	1961	1961
	South Africa	1910	1930	1994	
Asia	India	1950	1950	1950	1950
	Japan	1925	1955	1955	1955
	Indonesia	1955	1955	1955	1955
Oceania	Australia	1901 (united as a federation)	1902	1962	
	New Zealand	1879	1893	1879	1879

the ballot—in quadrennial elections when that office is on the ballot; gubernatorial candidates or those for US Senate are first in other elections.) So we need to be careful in the choice of elections when we are comparing turnout among countries (or regions, if that is an issue). Many countries handle all of these matters more simply than is the case in the United States, but the point is that turnout comparisons are difficult and should be judged with this complexity in mind.

We can say, without implying precision, that turnout among countries differs. And we know some of the factors that determine those differences. Presidential elections have a higher turnout than legislative elections, though how much higher depends on the country and on whether the elections happen at the same time or on separate days. Legislative elections in parliamentary democracies have higher turnout than they do in countries with presidential systems and a separation of powers. National elections have higher turnout than subnational elections, and those elections have higher turnouts than local elections.

We also know that the demographic composition of the electorate changes as turnout changes. Voters with lower income and less education are less likely to turn out than those with higher income and more education (these factors correlate in virtually all societies, albeit the inequality-turnout relationship is much weaker in some countries than it is in the United States). Almost by definition, nations with higher turnout have an electorate that is more representative of their total population than countries with lower turnout; and, as a consequence, the representative government in those democracies is more reflective of the views of the entire population than in low-turnout countries.

Policies intended to affect turnout

If we know that turnout is important in evaluating how effectively elections lead to representative government, what policies affect turnout, and in what ways? Polities make choices in several areas that affect turnout.

In order to vote, one must typically be recognized by election authorities as eligible. How does a voter get on the list of those eligible to vote in an election? The harder it is to get on the list, the less likely citizens are to register to vote, and, as a consequence, the more likely they are not to vote, and thus not have their interests reflected in an election.

A spectrum emerges—from those countries in which citizens are automatically registered to vote upon reaching voting age, to those in which registration is automatic but requires some action (which has other benefits to the registrant as well), to those that require some action that is itself compulsory, to states in which registration is voluntary. These differences—up until the final one—speak to different ways in which polities view voting: Is it a right or an obligation? However, in all of these cases, nearly all citizens end up on the voting rolls. That is not the case in countries with voluntary registration.

In Costa Rica, every child born there (and every new citizen upon granting of citizenship) is given an identification number. That number is permanent and does not require renewal. At the age of 12, Costa Rican youths are presented with an identification card, useful for all purposes, including free medical care. At 18 (or when immigrants become citizens), Costa Ricans must go to the Supreme Electoral Tribunal and receive an updated identification card, with a picture and basic biographical information, including the locale in which they will vote. Receiving this card is considered a rite of passage, not an obligation. The card, which Costa Ricans carry with them at most times, is used for all identification purposes, including opening a bank account, demonstrating one's age, obtaining medical care, and voting. All 18-year-old Costa Rican citizens are thus automatically registered to vote. No one falls off the voting roll because of failure to register.

Automatic registration similar to that in Costa Rica is common in democracies throughout much of Latin America, Africa, Europe, and Asia; about two-thirds of the world's democracies have some sort of automatic registration. But variations do exist. Costa Ricans must appear in person to receive their identification card; as stated, it is viewed as a right, not an obligation, but some action is needed. This is the case in most countries; that is, registration is automatic, but it requires some action that is voluntary.

In a number of democracies, including Argentina, Chile, Israel, and the Netherlands, voter registration is done automatically by the state, using existing state records. That is, all citizens are automatically registered to vote upon reaching the minimum voting age, which is 18 in the vast majority of the world's democracies. (Nine countries, several in Latin America, have a minimum age of 16, while the United Arab Emirates has the highest at age 25.)

In those other countries, citizens must take a positive step to have their names added to the list of voters. Usually this is done through a local office; registration must be current in order for one to vote. If one moves residency, re-registration is often required. Some countries—Ireland and Canada as examples— make registration easy. Canada even maintains a role of future voters, so that those aged 14 to 17 can have their names added in advance of the time they become eligible to vote. In countries with eased registration procedures, the necessity to register is rarely a barrier to voting. More than 90 percent of age-eligible Canadians have been registered to vote in recent elections. Those who are not are often those without permanent ties to a local community—or others who have moved about for one reason or another.

By contrast, just over 70 percent of age-eligible citizens of the United States register to vote. This number varies significantly by state, from the low of Arkansas, with only 62 percent of age-eligible voters registered, to Minnesota, with over 82 percent.

What factors account for the interstate differences? And why, even in the states with highest registration percentages, do approximately one in five eligible voters fail to register?

In part, these are both matters of culture. Some American states have long histories of active participation in governance; Minnesota is certainly one of those. But some do not. These cultural norms are often rooted in the historical immigration patterns that vary from state to state. States that were originally populated by immigrants from countries with strong civic cultures, like the Scandinavian countries, often adopt a participant civic culture; those states whose immigrants came from countries with less of a participatory culture tend to follow those patterns as well.

But the variation is also a measure of public policy. Registration laws vary by how frequently one must participate in order to stay registered, whether or not one has to re-register if one moves within the same geographic area, whether one can register online or must do so in person, whether or not one can register on Election Day or if some time must exist between registration and voting, or how available local registrars are for citizens to register. In recent years some locales have required government-issued photo identification in order for potential voters to register, which is an impediment for some people.

For many years state governments in the American South used voting laws to keep African American citizens, enfranchised after the Civil War, from exercising that hard-earned right. Those laws were eliminated through a series of Supreme Court cases and the landmark Voting Rights Act of 1965, one of the crowning achievements of the civil rights movement of the early 1960s. But the legacy of those restrictive laws persists to this day in conservative opposition to every effort to ease registration and voting.

This type of disenfranchisement may well be another case in which the United States is an outlier. For instance, while there is variation in terms of whether incarcerated individuals are eligible to vote, the United States is one of the few nations that do not automatically return the franchise to citizens who have been convicted of a serious crime, served their time, and been released. In the United States, 48 states ban convicted felons from voting, such that in 2022 an estimated 4.6 million Americans—2 percent of the voting-age population—were ineligible to vote.

Legal changes account for only some of the failure of citizens to register to vote. From decades of polling data in the United States, we know that level of political participation varies with socioeconomic status and interest in government. But the impact of governmental action on citizens' lives does not vary with these factors. Thus, the fact that voting is not a requirement of citizenship but rather a right of citizenship that might be more or less difficult to claim means that the electorate in polities with lower voter registration is unrepresentative of the public at large in predictable ways, and that the electorate speaks with an economically biased voice.

Compulsory voting

Approximately 25 countries in the world require citizens to vote in all or some elections. These range from the small (Costa Rica) to the very large (Brazil). The countries range from those high on any democracy scale (Australia) to those not so highly rated (Egypt). Half of the nations with compulsory voting are in Latin America; only four (Belgium, Bulgaria, Greece, and Luxembourg) are in Europe.

Advocates for mandatory voting argue that decisions made in a democracy in which everyone participates are inherently more legitimate. They argue that citizenship comes with certain responsibilities, including the responsibility to participate in one's own governance. In addition, those favoring compulsory voting claim that the act of voting and deciding for whom one is going to

Table 6. Existence of compulsory voting in a sample of countries

Region	Country	Compulsory voting?	Year introduced
North America	Canada	No	
	USA	No	
	Mexico	Yes*	1857
Central America	Costa Rica	Yes*	1959
South America	Colombia	No	
	Chile	Yes/No	1925–2012, then abolished
	Brazil	Yes	1932
Europe	United Kingdom	No	
	Ireland	No	
	France	Yes (Senate only)	1950s or 60s
	Germany	No	
	Sweden	No	
	Estonia	No	
Middle East	Israel	No	
Africa	Nigeria	No	
	Ghana	No	
	Kenya	No	
	South Africa	No	

Region	Country	Compulsory voting?	Year introduced
Asia	India	No	
	Japan	No	
	Indonesia	No	
Oceania	Australia	Yes	1924
	New Zealand	No	

vote implies that the citizens will become more educated on the issues of the day, in part because political parties will make direct appeals to all citizens, not just to the voting elite.

Those against compulsory voting counter these arguments with two principal responses. First, they argue that requiring voting violates the basic democratic tenet of freedom—that the citizenry should be free not to go to the polls if they so choose. They claim that government will be less legitimate if it is voted into office by citizens voting against their own will. (Technically, in countries with secret ballots, the requirement of compulsory voting means a citizen is required to go to the polls and collect a ballot, but no one can know whether, in the secrecy of the voting booth, that citizen decides to leave the ballot blank—that is, not to vote for any candidate.) Second, critics of compulsory voting claim that citizens not interested in politics and government will cast a vote without learning about candidates and issues—as a means of protesting the requirement; if they are not voting voluntarily, why would they educate themselves voluntarily? In addition, some claim that enforcing compulsory voting entails expenses that poorer democracies cannot afford.

The countries with compulsory voting hold less than 15 percent of the world's population. In recent years, only Bulgaria (2016) and Samoa (2019) have been added to the list of countries requiring citizens to vote.

How does one view high voter turnout more generally? If citizens vote because they care about their government and the decisions it makes on their behalf, that is a sign of a healthy democracy. If citizens vote because they are opposed to their government and want to change those who rule over them, that may be bad for incumbents, but that, too, is a sign of a healthy democracy.

What about low voter turnout? On the one hand, if citizens do not vote because they think the government and its policies are stacked against them and that it will not matter who wins, that is a bad sign for democracy. It is, in fact, a recipe for mass action against the government. However, if citizens do not vote because they are satisfied with the direction of the government and think they will continue to be satisfied no matter who wins an election, that is not necessarily a bad sign. Essentially, the nonvoters are making a cost-benefit analysis of the use of their time and concluding that, because they will be satisfied with whoever wins, they have better uses of their time than voting, especially if the cost of voting is high.

Frequency of voting

Compare the two pictures below. The first is of voters lined up to cast their ballots in one of the first elections held in South Africa after the end of apartheid. Lines were long, but the citizens were thrilled to be able to vote—and the queue, long as it was, seemed festive and joyous.

The second is the line outside a voting location in Marietta, Georgia, in the United States in 2020. The voters were angry that they had to wait, often for hours, to cast their ballot in the US presidential election. Rather than expressing joy at the chance to vote, they were upset that election officials had made it difficult to exercise their most basic right.

6. Voters in the first post-apartheid elections in South Africa in 1994 were eager to exercise their right to vote and were not deterred by long lines.

7. Voters in line in Marietta, Georgia, where they often had to wait for hours to vote.

The pictures are instructive for two reasons. First, they speak to incentives for voting. If voters are highly motivated, if the act of voting itself is of great value to them, they will walk long distances, wait in long lines, and endure whatever hardships are necessary to exercise the franchise. If the act of voting itself is novel, if it is a communal ritual, voters will sacrifice a great deal to engage in the process.

But if voting is intentionally made more difficult, if public officials attempt to dissuade people from voting, their efforts may succeed and citizens will be less likely to turn out, particularly if circumstances increase the cost of voting in terms of time and effort and inability to do other things. However, citizens will also resent these attempts to limit their franchise and, though upset, they may be willing to accept the hardships in order to register their will.

Beyond eligibility requirements, public policy can also affect turnout, at times intentionally and at times not. Voters in the United States are asked to go to the polls to cast ballots for candidates for more offices and more often than is true in any other nation. (The Swiss go to the polls more often, three to four times a year, but often to decide policies, not necessarily to elect officials.) Americans vote for president, US senators, and US representatives—the elected officials at the national level. They vote for governors, state legislators in two houses (in all states except Nebraska), and in some states officials in a variety of other statewide offices (secretaries of state, treasurers, auditors, judges, agriculture commissioners, etc.). They vote for county and local officials (commissioners, mayors, council members, but also water district commissioners, school board members, planning board members, etc.). In the United States, unusual but not unique among democracies, voters are also asked to go to the polls for intraparty primaries to select candidates to run for each of these offices. Though many individual seats are uncontested, voters are still asked to vote because nearly always at least some offices on the ballot feature contests for party nominations. In some American states they vote for all or most of these officials at the same time, casting what is called a "long ballot." In others, such as Kentucky, officials separate state and local elections from national elections, so that the voters can focus on state and local issues.

If electing the officials who govern citizen actions is a positive sign reflecting an effective democracy, can there be too much democracy? The move to elect a large number of officials in the United States was a reaction to cronyism and appointments by corrupt party leaders. But do citizens really know enough about officials down the ballot to make an informed choice? Do they really care? Falloff, the failure to cast any vote at all for elections down the ballot, is a consequence perhaps more of voter fatigue than voter apathy. They do not care enough to learn about these candidates, or even to stay in the voting booth long enough to cast a vote. Low turnout in local and state elections (and in primary elections for all offices) is another sign of voter fatigue. Voters in Baton Rouge, Louisiana, in the 2010s, were asked to go to the polls more than ten times in an average two-year period. They felt that was too many times—and turnout for local and state elections, often for the offices that affect the citizenry most directly, was consequently low.

The length of a term of office also affects how often citizens are asked to vote. In the United States, the president and most governors serve four-year terms, representatives in Congress and most state legislators serve two-year terms, and US senators serve six-year terms. That means that elections to important federal and state offices are held at least every two years. A new election seems to start as soon as the previous one is decided. Politicians may live and breathe for each election cycle—and the policy decisions made by those elected do have consequences for all citizens—but most citizens simply do not care about politics all the time. They tire. Life's everyday decisions—about work, about feeding and housing a family, about their kids' school, even about football matches and the latest movie and television show—are higher priorities. And voter fatigue mounts with the constant barrage of political appeals.

Voting

55

Table 7. Length of legislative terms in a sample of countries

Region	Country	Lower house	Upper house	Unicameral
North America	Canada	4 years or until election called	Age 75 or resignation	
	USA	2 years	6 years, but one-third elected every two years	
	Mexico	3 years	6 years	
Central America	Costa Rica			4 years
South America	Colombia	4 years	4 years	
	Chile	4 years	8 years	
	Brazil	4 years	8 years	
Europe	United Kingdom	5 years	Life or end of religious terms (bishops)	
	Ireland	5 years	5 years	
	France	5 years	6 years	

			Life or end of religious terms (bishops)
	Germany	4 years	
	Sweden		4 years
	Estonia		4 years
Middle East	Israel		4 years
Africa	Nigeria	4 years	4 years
	Ghana		4 years
	Kenya	5 years	5 years
	South Africa	5 years	Determined by provinces
Asia	India	5 years	6 years
	Japan	4 years	6 years
	Indonesia	5 years	5 years
Oceania	Australia	3 years	6 years, but not all at the same time
	New Zealand		3 years

Voting

The number of times citizens in the United States must go to the polls is an outlier. For instance, in France, the president and the National Assembly are elected to a five-year term, while municipal and regional elections are held every six years. The norm for lower houses is for terms to run four or five years, for upper houses for terms of five or six years, and for unicameral legislators to serve four-year terms. Similarly, most presidents around the world serve terms longer than that of the president of the United States. Many, such as the president of Costa Rica, are limited to one term in office, though some can run again after sitting out at least one term.

Most countries separate elections for one office from those for another. And most fill minor executive offices by appointment. The long ballot faced by voters in the United States is an anomaly, the result of a political reform movement more than a century ago. One unanticipated consequence of those democratizing reforms that led to more officials being chosen by voters is voter fatigue, a clear contributor to lower voter turnout in many elections.

When, where, and how people vote

Much of the controversy over voting in the 2020s concerns the administration of elections. Once again, policymakers can affect turnout. The first such issue deals with when elections are held. In the United States, Election Day for national and most state elections is the first Tuesday after the first Monday in November. Election Day is not a holiday, though many workers are given some time off to vote. Why November? Why a Tuesday? And why not the first Tuesday but rather the first Tuesday after the first Monday? As with many election laws, the historical reasons for establishing a date made sense, but little of that logic applies today.

Originally, American states set the dates for elections—and they were not held on the same day throughout the country. In the

mid-nineteenth century, however, the United States Congress
sought to have one day set aside for all elections. At the time, the
United States was a largely agrarian, deeply religious nation.
November was chosen because farmers were more likely to have
time to vote after the fall harvest. They needed time because,
before the day of the automobile, traveling by horse and buggy to
the nearest town took some time and effort. Tuesday was chosen
after Sunday was eliminated for religious reasons and Wednesday
because it was market day. Given these limitations, Tuesday
seemed the best choice. And why not the first Tuesday? That could
fall on November 1, All Saints' Day, again raising religious
objections. All of that made sense in the context of the times.
None of it does today.

More countries hold elections on Sundays than on any other day.
This is true in democracies throughout most of Europe, Asia, and
Latin America. The major exceptions are countries that are now
or once were part of the British Empire; as examples, the UK
holds elections on Thursdays, Australia and New Zealand on
Saturdays, Canada on Mondays, and Kenya on Tuesdays. A few
countries, such as Israel and Indonesia, hold elections on
weekdays but designate Election Day as a national holiday.

Does the day on which citizens vote make a difference? Sunday
has been chosen by most nations in order to make it easier for
citizens to vote without missing work. Polities that make Election
Day a holiday do so to increase turnout as well. Not only do fewer
people work on a holiday, but celebrating Election Day encourages
people to take part in a civic act, to feel national pride in voting.

Are there arguments against choosing Sunday or making Election
Day a holiday? The main argument against such a change in the
United States and elsewhere is that people will use the day for a
vacation or a trip to the beach or some such activity rather than
vote. In the past, large manufacturers have argued against a
holiday, as it would mean paying their employees more to work on

Voting

that day. None of these arguments rest on empirical evidence, only on conjecture. And again, those who prefer lower turnout are less likely to want a change; those who prefer higher turnout—for philosophical or political reasons—call for reform.

When Election Day is scheduled becomes less important if citizens are given options to vote on other days, either in person or remotely. Do people vote in person, by absentee ballot, by mail-in ballots, or in front of a computer? Again, various countries (and states within the United States) have adopted a range of options— and these have engendered considerable controversy.

The goal of all of these options is to facilitate voting by those who might have trouble going to the polls on one Election Day. Absentee or postal voting, a system through which a citizen can vote without actually going to the polls, has been used in the United States for more than a century. Absentee voting was implemented to assist those unable to travel to the polls—the sick, the elderly—or those who were unavoidably away from their polling place on Election Day—such as those who travel for work, members of the military, or students. The controversy arises over whether one must have a reason for voting absentee or whether one can do so simply as a matter of convenience. The latter option obviously makes voting easier than does the former.

Before the COVID-19 pandemic, about 15 countries had some variety of absentee voting practices. However, during the COVID-19 pandemic, many more adopted at least temporary measures to allow citizens to vote without the necessity of traveling to a polling place and exposing themselves to possible infection. Whether these practices will be extended after the pandemic is unknown; they would undoubtedly help people to exercise their right to vote.

An extension of no-excuse absentee voting would be eliminating in-person Election Day voting altogether and having everyone vote by mail. The mechanism would be quite simple: election officials mail a ballot to every registered voter, and voters fill out the ballot whenever they want and either mail it back in (with variation in who pays for the return postage) or drop it off at a designated spot. The obvious advantage of this system is that it makes voting very easy for any citizen: you vote from the comfort of your own home. The disadvantage cited by critics is that there is no check on who actually fills out the ballot; they claim it is an invitation to fraud. Advocates of voting by mail counter that no fraud has been exposed in the jurisdictions that have been using this system for many election cycles.

Another option allows for early voting. A number of countries or regions within countries "open the polls" before Election Day so that those unable to vote or inconvenienced by voting on Election Day can do so in advance. Several countries allow early voting for some voters; only a few, including Canada, offer it to all voters. In some countries, particularly those with many citizens living long distances from polling places, elections extend over a period of days as a routine practice. One could argue that this is the equivalent to absentee voting in person. Again, the advantage is obvious. If polls are open earlier and for more hours, those for whom casting a ballot during a set period of time on one day is difficult can do so more easily. The disadvantage here is cost. Someone must be present at some location to hand out ballots and to receive them. In addition, those who vote early might later regret that vote, as some campaign revelation or a late-breaking event might alter how they would have voted. Experience with early voting proves that this option increases turnout; critics argue that the practice should be limited to reduce the cost and to assure that voters have exposure to as much information as possible before casting their votes.

As more and more citizens have access to the Internet, election officials have considered online voting. The advantage, like voting by mail, is ease of access; online voting is particularly appealing to those living in remote areas, where travel to a central polling place might be as difficult as it was when citizens had to travel many miles on horseback to cast their ballots. However, many argue that online voting should not be implemented until Internet access and use are universal, lest there be an inherent economic bias implied by its use. And skeptics fear that online voting is too easily compromised by hackers, threatening the security of the ballot. Since 2007, e-voting has been used in Estonia's parliamentary elections. Estonians may vote six to eight days prior to Election Day. As a result, turnout has increased, and no negative consequences have been noted.

As important as when and how votes are cast is to voter turnout, accessibility issues are equally significant. One of the advantages of postal voting is that citizens do not have to travel long distances to exercise their right to vote, nor do they need to sacrifice a great deal of their time. But most countries do not permit such voting. In many lower-income democracies, for instance, citizens must travel long distances over poor roads in order to vote. Clearly these constraints have an impact on turnout.

So, too, do issues of literacy and language differences. When comparing practices in various countries, one must explore whether lower-literacy citizens are given the opportunity to vote, and, if so, how. The same is true in countries in which segments of the population do not speak or read the national language. Are ballots printed in various languages? Are there pictures or symbols printed on ballots to inform voters who cannot read the dominant language?

These practices involve policy choices by public officials who want to either encourage or discourage those needing accommodations in order to vote to have that opportunity. Nowhere has that been more evident than in the post–Civil War American South, where freed slaves, whose right to vote was acknowledged in the Fifteenth Amendment to the US Constitution, were prevented from exercising that right. They were constrained from voting through a series of laws, known as Jim Crow laws, that were designed to prevent Black Americans from voting. These laws included but were not limited to placing polling places in areas of a district far from where African Americans lived, requiring poll taxes, instituting literacy tests that were administered unevenly to keep this group out of the electorate, and opening the polls only during hours when most laborers had to be at work. Low turnout among former slaves and their descendants from the time the Fifteenth Amendment was ratified in 1870 until the passage of the Voting Rights Act of 1965 (which took power over these matters out of state hands and placed it under federal control, and which led to vastly increased Black turnout) provides ample empirical evidence that electoral rules and practices have a clear impact on who turns out to vote.

Accessibility versus security

One overriding theme emerges as we examine the public policy options regarding voting. Polities have to weigh two conflicting values. On the one hand, democracies should want citizens to vote so that they can express their views on the policies of the day and the performance of those who govern. That is the most basic tenet of democratic governance. And that value argues for ease of access to the ballot, making it possible for citizens to participate in self-governance.

On the other hand, one could also stress the security of the ballot. Only those who are eligible to vote (however that is defined in any polity) should cast ballots that are counted. No one should vote more than once. Voters should cast their own ballots, and no one should pressure them into voting a certain way. Those ineligible to vote should not receive ballots. Implementation of these principles in turn requires that election officials are able to monitor voting carefully.

This trade-off between ease of access to the ballot and security of the ballot is present in all of the policy options—ease of or control over registration, when one votes, how one votes, where one votes, how one's eligibility to vote is confirmed. Election officials struggle with this dilemma, but people of good will should be able to come to acceptable compromises on these issues, if all one were concerned about was balancing these two basic values. However, more is involved, as these decisions also have clear political implications.

Who votes defines who is represented

Political scientists have long argued that there is a systematic difference between voters and nonvoters. Voters are more interested in politics, are more informed about political issues and the views of candidates, and care more about the outcome of elections. Those for whom politics and voting seems more important participate more. None of that should be surprising.

But we also know that these factors vary, along with others that are more troubling. There is an inherent economic bias in political participation. Those who are wealthier, more educated, or more tied to the ruling class in any society are more likely to participate, whether that participation is defined as learning about politics, being actively involved in politics, or simply voting. The electorate does not reflect the larger society in terms of education, wealth, or social status.

It follows logically that those who are chosen by an unrepresentative electorate govern in a way that favors those who have selected them. One example will suffice to demonstrate this point. Everyone agrees that homelessness is a problem in virtually every society, yet it is a problem that is rarely addressed as a top governmental priority. Why? There are many reasons, but surely one is that the homeless do not participate in governance and mostly do not vote. Few political leaders see it as being in their self-interest to champion the homeless and, in crassest terms, to tax their constituents to provide services to those who do not participate in governing.

Voting is an act that requires the citizen to make some level of effort. For those who have less leisure time, that effort is more costly. They have to give up time at work or some of their free time in order to vote. And many choose not to do so. That mere fact goes a long way toward explaining variations in voting turnout by education and income. It also explains why changing laws to ease access to the ballot is not a politically neutral decision. Political parties that represent less powerful classes in society, such as the poor and minorities, argue for ease of access to ballots. Those who benefit from support by the privileged in society "worry" about security of the ballot, which some define as voting by those arguing for fundamental changes in society. Voting is an inherently political act. So, too, is easing or restricting access to the ballot. How these issues are resolved goes a long way toward determining who is represented in any nation's government.

Chapter 4
Administering elections

On January 2, 2021, President Donald Trump telephoned Brad Raffensperger, the secretary of state of Georgia, and asked him to review the results of the presidential election in Georgia one more time. Raffensperger had already overseen three recounts, but Trump said, "I just want to find, uh, 11,780 votes," which happened to be the exact number he would have needed to exceed President Biden's total in Georgia.

Trump called Raffensperger, because in Georgia the secretary of state administers elections and has control over any recounts. The Trump campaign made similar calls in other states in which the election results were close, not always to secretaries of state, but to whoever ran that state's elections.

Campaigns have to be aware of how elections are run in any polity, and by whom. Only with that knowledge of local circumstances can they understand how elections are run and who, if anyone, can question an outcome. Who oversees voting and vote counting? Additionally, who determines the delimitation of the boundaries of electoral districts? How are election campaigns run? What role do political parties play in candidate selection and campaigning? How are campaigns financed, and are there limitations on campaign spending or activities? How are voters informed about their choices? What role does the state play in regulating election campaigns and other political communication? What about civic education? What role do the media play? How are the media regulated, if at all? What is the role and influence of paid media versus free or earned media? Together, these dimensions set the stage for elections and affect public perceptions of the fairness of the election process and the credibility of election outcomes.

Managing elections

Electoral administration involves regulating the most political of activities. In many countries, partisan actors understand the political implications of the decisions made in administering elections and strive to control them. Nowhere has this been more evident than in the United States during and after the Trump presidency. In the American federal system, each individual state is responsible for managing elections, including those for the national legislature and for the president. The states, therefore, have become targets of partisan politics, including attempts to pressure election officials or to ensure that one party or the other has the upper hand.

However, in other countries, in fact in the vast majority of democracies, these consequential decisions concerning the administration of the most political of acts—democratically electing those who govern—have been taken out of politics and are made by appointed experts. These election managers and election management bodies (EMBs) could be appointed by the executive or the legislature, or they could even come from within the executive, as in many Western European democracies where election managers are civil servants. The most common type of election managers, however, are independent bodies. Some EMBs are accountable to the executive, others to the judiciary.

The Chief Electoral Officer in Canada is appointed on the basis of acknowledged expertise and serves a ten-year term. The seven members of the Superior Electoral Tribunal in Brazil are experts appointed to staggered terms by a consensus reached by judges and elected officials in various offices. The five-member National Election Commission in Iceland is composed of experts appointed to staggered four-year terms by the legislature. Kenya's seven-member Independent Electoral and Boundaries Commission, composed of election experts, is appointed by a special Selection Committee chosen by the president and the legislature. Most of these commissions have independent authority, separate from that of the sitting government; most of the multimember commissions appoint their own chairs, often the most powerful figure in the process. However appointed, EMBs are responsible for all or some of the following activities: determining electoral districts, voter registration, voter education, regulating campaigns, conducting elections, counting votes, and adjudicating disputes that arise during the electoral process.

Electoral districts

An electoral district, or voting district, is a geographical area that is represented in the legislature by a seat in a single-member district (SMD) or by some number of seats in a multimember district (MMD). Voters registered in a particular district may vote only in that district. How are electoral districts delimited, and how are they reapportioned to reflect changes in population? And how are seats, or representatives, apportioned among the districts? Who makes these decisions, using what rules or criteria?

Using preexisting governmental or administrative units as the district from which to choose representatives to a national legislature is relatively easy and draws on citizen loyalty to those areas. A town or a county or a region means more to a citizen than does an electoral district that is redrawn every time a shift in population is reflected in new lines. Often citizens in these existing units have certain interests in common; certainly they have shared histories and societal norms. Using these preexisting lines avoids the problem of drawing district boundaries to benefit or harm a specific party or candidate—one of the most vexing problems facing politicians in the United States.

Apportionment is the process of distributing seats in the legislature among administrative units, districts, or states. For example, if a country has one million citizens, and there are 100 seats in the national legislature, each legislator represents 10,000 citizens. If legislators are chosen in SMDs, as in the United States, one person–one vote mandates that each district have a population of 10,000 citizens. If legislators are elected in MMDs with proportional representation (PR), a district with 3 representatives should have 30,000 citizens; one with 5 representatives, 50,000; and so on. (There can be a difference between citizens and voters. Citizens below a certain age are not eligible to vote; and some countries or regions within countries impose other restrictions on who can vote. In apportioning representatives equally, the denominator most often used is citizens, but a state could easily make other choices.)

Of course, because districts are apportioned at one point in time, some inequality follows from citizens moving from one district to another, and from births and deaths, but that is unavoidable. Apportioning representatives among the districts in a legislature requires an accurate count of the population, or at least of citizens or registered voters. Apportionment can be based on a periodic population census, usually every five to ten years, or by using electoral rolls.

Apportioning legislators among districts of equal population works in those countries that draw district lines for the purpose of creating equal-sized districts. But what about those countries that use existing administrative or governmental units? In those cases, the population of the preexisting districts is known, and the number of representatives is apportioned accordingly. However, apportioning representatives while maintaining existing lines leads to increased inequality, as variation in the population of the districts is often greater than variation in the number of representatives apportioned to each. All of which is to say that apportioning representatives to guarantee equal vote power is not the simple arithmetic process it might appear to be.

Much of the controversy over drawing district lines after the decennial censuses in the United States revolves around redistricting, not reapportionment. The number of representatives a state elects to the House of Representatives is determined by a mathematical formula that has been in use since 1941. Mathematicians have long fought over which specific formula for apportionment is fairest, but politicians seem satisfied not to change the one in use. After each census, mathematicians in one state or another write articles showing how their state would have received one more representative were a different formula used, often with reference back to the formula suggested by Thomas Jefferson for the first apportionment. However, because these arguments are extremely esoteric and technical, and because normally only one state has a real interest in any change, politicians have left well enough alone after the last eight censuses.

But how the district lines are to be drawn within each state is a very different matter. In 25 US states, district boundaries are drawn by state legislatures. Thirteen states have independent commissions for that purpose, while five states have independent commissions whose work is reviewed by the legislature, and one has a small group of politicians draw its lines; six states have only one congressional district and do not need boundary commissions. The term "gerrymandering" refers to drawing district lines in order to gain an electoral advantage for a particular party or candidate. Gerrymandering is nearly as old as the country; the term was coined after Governor Elbridge Gerry of Massachusetts signed into law a redistricting bill in 1812 that helped his party retain its majority, with one district ostensibly shaped like a salamander.

8. The term "gerrymander" was suggested in this 1812 cartoon in the *Boston Gazette*, which satirized the legislative districts drawn by Massachusetts governor Eldridge Gerry after the 1810 census.

Gerrymandering has a negative connotation today, but that does not keep partisan legislatures from drawing seats that help their co-partisans. The United States Supreme Court has refused to prohibit partisan gerrymandering, citing the constitutional provision that gives that power to the states. Thus, after the last reapportionment following the 2020 census, the Supreme Court allowed redistricting schemes drawn up by partisan legislatures clearly to benefit their party to stand; the justices claimed that the states, not the federal government, had the right to draw district lines, unless those lines violated some federal law, such as the Civil

Rights Act. The Pennsylvania Supreme Court, relying on its state's constitution, not the federal constitution, outlawed partisan gerrymandering in that state, but only in that state. Reformers, who have long argued that partisan gerrymandering is one of the most egregious practices denying citizens fair representation, have taken hope from this ruling that an avenue to end the practice might exist. Citizens of various states, including Arizona, California, Michigan, and New York, have not waited for judicial action but have instead taken the redistricting power away from their legislatures and given it to citizen boards, selected in various ways, to reduce partisan bias.

The process of elections

In some countries, an EMB decides the date of the next general election. In parliamentary systems, the government of the day can call the next election, or in some cases, if the government has lost a vote of confidence in the parliament, new elections are called, often with only a few weeks to prepare. In other countries, such as the United States, the legislative term is fixed and the date of the election is set by law.

Each country has its own legal requirements for candidacy, normally based on age and citizenship, and procedures for becoming an official candidate. In parliamentary systems, political parties typically control candidate selection in SMDs and determine the party lists for PR elections. For that reason, independent or unaffiliated candidates are relatively unusual in parliamentary democracies. Ireland is an exception to this norm because of its use of the single transferable vote (STV) method, a process of voting and counting votes that opens the door to the candidacy of popular independents by allowing voters to rank all candidates, regardless of party affiliation or independent status.

One legendary mid-nineteenth-century American politician, Boss Tweed of Tammany Hall (in New York), claimed with pride,

"I don't care who does the electing, just so I do the nominating." The implication was clear: choosing who had access to a place on the ballot was the most important power in politics at the time. And in some nations, this is still the case, though in democracies that power is no longer controlled by one person. But the role of party is one of the key factors that differentiate democracies from each other.

Political scientists deem parties to be weak or strong according to a number of criteria. Strong political parties tend to have permanent and professional organizations, they tend to control the nominating process, and they have a great deal of influence over how their members vote in the legislature. Thus, in a strong party system, the leader in the legislature can demand support from party members on key votes, with the threat that those members who oppose the leader will not be running on the party ballot in the next election. Party discipline is critical for these parties, which tend to be programmatic and in almost all cases highly centralized. Thus, when the prime minister of the United Kingdom requires that his or her party members support the government's position on a key vote, a demand colorfully described as "whipping the members," the legislators will comply or the government may well fall.

Compare that to the situation in a relatively weak party system such as that in the United States. What party discipline exists is a result of shared values, not pressure from the leader. In 2022, when Senator Joe Manchin of West Virginia defied the Democratic Party on votes critical to gaining approval for President Biden's key programs, Democratic Party Majority Leader Chuck Schumer (NY) had no power to force compliance. Manchin argued, accurately, that he was reflecting the views of his constituents in West Virginia, and that those voters, not Schumer, would determine if he would continue to represent them. In a decentralized party system, with nominations controlled in local areas in primary elections, national leaders can exert relatively little influence.

The primary system is often listed as one of the main causes of the extreme polarization of American politics. Turnout in primary elections tends to be very low, and those at the political extreme—right-wing conservatives in the Republican Party and left-wing liberals in the Democratic Party—turn out in higher numbers and thus influence primary outcomes. As a result, nominees tend to come more from the parties' ideological extremes. When national leaders try to influence legislators, the legislators, protecting their own re-election chances, are often concerned that they will face primary competition if they appear too accommodating. They therefore resist entreaties to compromise and back positions deemed to be more ideologically pure. Furthermore, it is a system out of the control of national party leaders that breeds extremist candidates, and thus extremist officeholders.

Parties have resources other than control over nominations. Parties structure the battle for power, and citizens evaluate candidates based on party affiliation. Parties develop platforms that explain their core values and policy priorities, and they create election manifestos to let voters know how they differ from other parties, and also what their plans would be for governing. Parties determine the message for elections, and the perception of how party leaders are governing (or opposing those in government) determines how voters cast their ballots. On this point, the electoral process in the United States is an outlier, with clear consequences for how the nation is governed.

Countries vary in terms of how long campaigns are contested, who pays for the messages that are transmitted (the government, the parties, or the candidates), and whether those messages are regulated. They also vary in terms of who manages and funds election campaigns, and whether political parties determine the messages that reach voters or if individual candidates are more determinative of their own campaigns.

In a number of countries, the length of campaigns is set in law. In Japan, where political campaigns are highly regulated, the official campaign period is only 12 days. France's two-round presidential election is completed very quickly. There is only a month between the date on which candidates are certified and the first round of the presidential election—and only two additional weeks until the second round. Argentina allows political advertising only in the two months before an election. Mexican law declares that campaigning can go on only 90 days before an election (and 60 days before that to determine nominees). In Nigeria, campaigns may not exceed 150 days.

In a sense, the law also determines the length of presidential campaigns in the United States. The First Amendment to the US Constitution guarantees freedom of speech, with political speech protected to the extreme. Because of that constitutional provision, no law can restrict campaigning for president. For most of the nation's history, all campaigning was done within the calendar

9. In many countries, such as Nigeria, there is a legal limit to how long election posters may be displayed.

year of an election, but since the 1980s, the campaign period has expanded and expanded—to the point that both President Biden and former president Trump announced their intentions to run in 2024 (though neither made an official declaration, as that would have imposed campaign finance limitations) during 2021, the first year of Biden's term. Of course, nothing says that they cannot change their minds—and, as a result, many other candidates began testing the political waters in states with early nominating contests more than two years before those contests were to be held.

Representatives in the US House complain that they are always campaigning. Their campaigns for re-election literally begin right after the votes are counted. Even those from the West Coast return from Washington to their districts almost every weekend. They spend hours each week on the phone raising money whenever they are in Washington. A good representative should always stay in touch with constituents, but in the case of those serving in Congress, campaigning is never far from their minds. In recent years this phenomenon has spread from the US House of Representatives to the Senate, even though senators serve six-year terms.

But who pays attention to campaigning that goes on far in advance of an election? The audience for early campaigning in the United States is the political elite who judge whether a potential candidate is a serious contender. The purpose of early campaigning—during the so-called invisible primary—is not to persuade voters but to persuade political leaders and donors that a potential candidate can be successful.

According to data gathered by the ACE Electoral Knowledge Network, in most democracies, political parties control some, if not all, campaign funding. In 68 percent of countries worldwide, the state provides free or subsidized media access to parties. In other cases, parties are able to raise more money—or to coordinate the donation of campaign funds—in ways that individual candidates cannot. Candidates, even in countries with weak party systems, understand the incentive to go along if they want help in future campaigns.

The principle behind in-kind, state support is equity. Sometimes all parties have access to public funds, while in others access and the generosity of support are contingent on a party's electoral performance in the previous election. In some countries' elections, there is a legal maximum ceiling on campaign expenses. States not only provide funds, but sometimes they also make space available for campaigning--such as for election rallies, information booths, or to hang posters, placards, and billboards. A significant element of state support for election campaigns is the availability of free or subsidized broadcast time on state/public media and the enforcement of the principle of neutrality. Some countries, like France and the United Kingdom, prohibit paid broadcasting, while other countries limit it, and still others, like the United States, have no limitations. In almost every country, political parties are sponsors of campaign ads for legislative candidates, whereas in the United States the candidates are the sponsors of their own ads.

Whether private contributions from individuals, corporations, and interest groups are permitted, and whether such contributions must be disclosed, are other features of the administration of elections. If contributions are permitted but need not be disclosed, citizens have no way of knowing what individuals or organizations have influence over elected officials. If, however, such contributions must be disclosed, candidates can make the identity of their opponents' supporters a campaign issue. And, if private contributions are not permitted, candidates owe allegiance only to their political party and their supporters. The influence of private money and private interests over public policy varies accordingly.

During campaigns, the candidates and the parties try to communicate messages to voters about how things are going and what they would do differently. In most countries, campaign messages are put forth by the parties—sometimes funded by the government, sometimes not. Again, the United States is the outlier. In US presidential and congressional elections, candidates can and do spend as much money as they can raise, literally hundreds of millions of dollars. And the First Amendment protects their right to do so. Furthermore, they can say anything they want, and the Supreme Court has ruled that even lies are protected political speech.

Compare that to France, where presidential candidates are limited to spending only about 16 million euros, and another 6 million if they qualify for the runoff. Or to Brazil, where candidates cannot advertise on television. Or to those countries in which parties produce campaign material in a specified format that is distributed to all potential voters by the state.

Political consulting is a huge industry in those countries that permit unlimited political communication on some or all media, but nowhere is it as dominating as in the United States. There, much of that advertising is negative in tone—and many citizens resent it. But we also know that negative messages get through and affect how citizens view candidates who are attacked. Culture and history influence societal attitudes about negative campaign advertising. In Germany, for instance, a legacy of the intense propaganda during the Nazi dictatorship has resulted in a strong cultural distaste for negative political campaigning. Also, in multiparty and parliamentary systems, where one party rarely wins enough seats to form a majority government on its own, the prospect of coalition-building after the election discourages the kind of negativity one associates with American-style campaigning.

What information do citizens need to make informed judgments in an election, and how do they get that information? Political scientist V. O. Key Jr. colloquially claimed that all citizens needed

Table 8. Regulations on funding and spending in a sample of countries

Region	Country	Public funding of parties	Free or subsidized access to media for political parties	Allow paid political advertising
North America	Canada	Yes	Yes	Yes, but within limits
	United States	No	No	Yes
	Mexico	Yes	Yes	Yes (commercial, not public, TV)
Central America	Costa Rica	Yes	No	Yes
South America	Colombia	Yes	Yes	
	Chile	Yes	Yes	No
	Brazil	Yes (but little)	Yes	No
Europe	United Kingdom	Yes	Yes	No
	Ireland	Yes	No	No
	France	Yes	Yes	No
	Germany	Yes	Yes	Yes (commercial, not public, TV)

(continued)

Table 8. Continued

Region	Country	Public funding of parties	Free or subsidized access to media for political parties	Allow paid political advertising
	Sweden	Yes	Yes	No
	Estonia	Yes	Yes	Yes (commercial, not public TV)
Middle East	Israel	Yes	Yes	Yes
Africa	Nigeria	No	No	Yes
	Ghana	No	Yes	Yes
	Kenya	Yes	No	
	South Africa	Yes	Yes	Yes
Asia	India	No	No	Yes
	Japan	Yes	No	Yes (commercial, not public, TV)
	Indonesia	Yes	No	Yes
Oceania	Australia	Yes	Yes	Yes (commercial, not public, TV)
	New Zealand	Yes	No	Yes (with limits)

to know to evaluate those who were governing was whether their shoes were pinching. If their shoes were pinching, if prices were high, if services were not available, or if the nation was under threat, then citizens blamed those in power. If people were comfortable, safe, and secure, they credited those in power. It did not matter if citizens were informed about the details of government policy, they intuitively knew whether they were pleased with the outcomes or not—and that was all they needed to vote. Political scientists call this "retrospective voting," voting based on what the government has done. Not much citizen effort is needed to gain this kind of information.

At a minimum, voters should be informed by the government about how and where to register, where polling sites are located and what hours they operate, what candidates and parties are running, and what offices or referenda or ballot initiatives are being decided. This information should be accessible to all, posted on the website of the EMB, if a country has one, and broadcast on public service announcements on various mass media and in various languages, where relevant.

Some countries take civic education very seriously. Germany, for instance, has a federal agency for civic education. It provides assistance to teachers and offers many materials at no charge to teachers, students, and the general public. Similarly, Mexico's Federal Election Institute is charged with assisting in the development of extensive education about democracy, not just at election time. In some countries, voter education is a task of EMBs, often complemented by voter information efforts carried out by media, political parties, nongovernmental organizations, and through public education. Australia, Canada, and South Africa are countries where voter education is mandated by law and carried out by their EMBs.

Another fundamental task of election administration is counting votes. To ensure that all votes are counted accurately and transparently, countries have laws specifying how, when, and by whom votes are counted, tabulated, and reported. Poll workers are usually flanked by representatives of various stakeholders, namely political parties, candidates, and election observers. In many countries, the counting of votes is overseen by an independent EMB. Vote counting usually occurs immediately at each polling place. Sometimes there are special counting centers where votes are brought to be counted, though the transportation of ballots must be secure.

Various types of voting machines have been devised to ease the process, speed the counting, and reduce the chance of error or fraud. However, the norm globally is still to cast a paper ballot. Electronic voting machines are used in only about 10 percent of all countries. Voting machines fall into three categories: lever machines, in which the voter pulls a lever next to the desired candidates' names and the machine records the vote; punch cards for voting, in which the voter punches a hole next to the name of the favored candidates and votes are tabulated by machine; and optical mark scanners, in which the voter marks a ballot and a scanner reads the result into a computer.

Each type of machine has a problem. For instance, there is no paper trail on lever machines, which were most prominent during the mid-twentieth century, so observers cannot tell if the machines were altered between the voting and the counting. Punch cards are open to misreading, as was amply demonstrated by the controversy over "hanging chads" during the recount of the 2000 US presidential election in Florida. Citizens fear that any kind of computer counting can be hacked, which has led to calls for a paper trail even for computer-generated and counted ballots. As the British playwright Sir Tom Stoppard put it, "It's not the voting that's democracy, it's the counting." If the citizens fear that the counting is not done fairly, they will not trust the electoral system.

But to a great extent the fear of fraud in the counting of ballots is another problem that affects American elections, and thankfully not one shared by citizens of many nations other than the United States. The fear of fraud grew from the actions of legendary and corrupt political bosses who dominated many sections of the United States for more than a century. Mayor Richard Daley of Chicago, described in journalist Mike Royko's oft-cited book *Boss*, was reputed to have ordered votes counted from people long since dead, based on how they would have voted. It probably never happened, but legends tend to persist. In modern US politics the fear of fraud has been spread by false statements issued by former president Donald Trump after his 2020 loss to Joe Biden. Though no evidence of fraud has been produced, Trump has repeated his lies often enough that literally millions of his followers believe his charges to be true.

Is there a model electoral process?

The electoral process differs greatly from one modern democracy to the next. In the third decade of the twenty-first century, however, many citizens are dissatisfied with the way elections are run in their own country. Nowhere is this more true than in the United States. A study of 170 countries over 500 elections spanning 2012 to 2021 found that the United States ranked lowest among liberal democracies in perceptions of election integrity. It ranked 75th overall and 15th out of 29 countries in the Americas. The most satisfied countries in the Americas were Canada and Uruguay; in Europe, Finland, Sweden, and Denmark, followed closely by Estonia; in Africa, South Africa and Namibia; in Asia, Taiwan, Japan, and Korea; and in Oceania, New Zealand.

Because of this range in satisfaction with elections, we urge citizens to look at other systems with an open eye. What can citizens of one nation learn from the experience of citizens in another? In the United States, where state systems vary significantly, what can citizens of one state learn from the experience of those living elsewhere? Are there some common lessons citizens, reform advocates, and political leaders in all polities can draw about the core elements of elections? Even this brief exploration of elections suggests that greater independence for election managers and improving transparency about campaign funding and spending can enhance the integrity of elections. Liberal democracies, moreover, tend toward increasing voter eligibility and access to polls. Finally, because elections are increasingly challenged by cyberattacks and disinformation campaigns from inside and outside their countries, improving voter education and devoting greater resources to protecting the integrity of voting systems are necessary.

Chapter 5
Why electoral systems matter

Rules matter. In terms of electoral systems, both general system features and their specific rules and caveats can have important impacts on other political institutions, the nature of governance, and the public policies adapted in a country, whether they are characterized by strong partisanship or by consensus-seeking. Electoral rules also create incentives that shape the perceptions and behaviors of various actors, including voters, candidates for office, and elected officials.

Electoral systems, it is important to remember, are themselves shaped by incentives—those of their architects. Designers of electoral systems usually prioritize one set of objectives over another. Some designers (particularly those who will benefit, but also those looking for a system that makes citizen participation easy) prefer systems that are simple for voters and election administrators and have decisive election outcomes. In these electoral systems, one candidate is elected per district, and the candidate with the most votes wins. That winner, the thinking goes, possesses a strong mandate. In parliamentary systems, simplicity carries over to government formation, producing (typically) a two-party system, so that the winning party can form a single-party government rather than a coalition government. Simplicity and decisiveness, proponents argue, lead to strong and responsible government, where it is clear to voters who won, who governs, and whom to reward or punish in the next election.

The downside to this set of objectives and outcomes is that candidates may win the election or a parliamentary seat with a minority of the vote, in which case there is a manufactured majority government that may leave many voters feeling as if their vote was wasted, and that the policies that are likely to arise from the newly elected official/parliament will not represent their best interests or desires.

Another set of incentives and objectives, in contrast, will prioritize the faithful reflection of society in elected offices, fairness to smaller parties, and a style of government formation and governance that emphasizes cooperation and consensus. When representativeness is a priority, electoral systems may have more complicated formulas for translating votes into seats. Similarly, government formation may take more time and require negotiations between political parties, so coalition governments are often necessary. Fewer voters may feel that they have wasted their votes, and a broader swath of the public may trust that policymaking will reflect their needs and desires when the legislature mirrors the groups in society, but decision-making may be more challenging and might even produce less stable governments.

When electoral systems were designed in many older democracies, the general public's support for the systems was not necessarily a factor. Rather, the designers of electoral systems likely sought to protect their own status and to perpetuate the status quo. When noblemen gave up power to elected representatives, they typically designed systems that would allow them to keep as much of their power as possible. As new democracies have emerged, from independence movements or from transitions from authoritarianism, questions of electoral system design have not only benefited from learning about the experiences, including reforms, of established systems, but have also entailed a more deliberative process of constitutional design. The public's perception of the rules is harder to ignore, and the issue of fairness is more pressing today than it was in the eighteenth or nineteenth centuries, when former English colonies adopted plurality (FPTP) systems for legislative elections.

Elections and electoral rules can influence whether people believe they are fairly represented by their elected officials. People may evaluate representativeness in more than one way. For example, how accurately are their opinions and preferences represented by the people elected to office in their district? While it may be easier to evaluate preference representation in a system where people vote for a single candidate and only one person wins a seat, it is also possible—and common—that such elections produce winners with less than a majority, thereby wasting votes for other candidates. In that case, only a segment of the voters' preferences will be represented, whereas in a system based on proportionality, especially where there in a high district magnitude, a truer reflection of ideological views and policy preferences is likely to result.

Another way of evaluating representation is to examine demographic representation, or how faithfully elected institutions reflect the groups in society. Electoral rules and systems create or restrict access to aspiring candidates for office, thereby influencing the type of candidates that emerge. The rules of the game also affect how easy or difficult it is for candidates from third or minor parties to be elected. Because proportional representation (PR) and mixed systems have higher levels of this type of representation, those systems are often recommended for countries characterized by various kinds of diversity, as well as postconflict societies, where inclusivity and consensus-building are prioritized over majoritarianism and an adversarial style of politics. Where women's inclusion and minority representation are of importance, PR and mixed systems are likely to be favored, since parties have control over their lists and can deliberately place women and minorities on the list—and higher on the list to maximize their chances of election. Some parties even have gender quotas, placing women in every other spot on the party list, which is more typical of closed party lists that cannot be changed by voters. Over 60 countries around the world—not counting the United States—have political parties with voluntary gender quotas. Where PR elections feature low district magnitude, and certainly in single-member district systems (FPTP, TRS), candidates considered likely to win, or "safe," are often favored, and those candidates have traditionally come from dominant groups in society.

Electoral systems can also affect the decisiveness of elections. Decisive elections are products of simple ballots, where a voter casts one vote for one candidate, and there is a simple formula for translating votes into seats, that of winner-take-all. The problem with that simplicity, however, is it can distort the outcome of the election, and thus the seat composition in parliament. As the following table shows, the winner in a plurality, FPTP system like the UK's may not have a majority of the votes in their district, only a plurality, but they are elected anyway. The table shows the much higher level of electoral distortion—the difference between the share of national votes and the share of parliamentary seats awarded—in the British FPTP system as compared to the German mixed-member proportional (MMP) system.

Table 9. Distortion effects: Comparison of FPTP in the UK and MMP in Germany*

	Percentage of votes	Percentage of seats	Percentage of difference
UK (total 650 seats)			
Conservatives*	42.3	48.8	+6.5
Labour	40	40.3	+0.3

Liberal Democrats	7.37	1.8	−5.57
Greens	1.63	0.15	−1.48

Total Distortion: 13.88

Germany (709 seats)

Christian Democrats*	26.8	28.2	+1.4
Social Democrats*	20.5	21.6	+1.1
Liberals	10.8	11.3	+0.5
Greens	8.94	9.4	+0.46

Total Distortion: 3.46

* The parties marked with an asterisk (*) are those in the government formed following the election. The Conservatives in Britain formed a coalition with the Democratic Unionist Party. The coalition in Germany included the Bavarian sister party of the CDU (Christian Democratic Union), the CSU (Christian Socialist Union).

Turning to elections of the executive, we see similar distortion in the United States, where the winner-take-all aspect of the Electoral College system often (but not always) creates an artificially large majority for the incoming president. However, if one candidate wins a majority of the electoral votes, by small margins in most states, and the other wins a minority of the votes in states won by large margins, the Electoral College system distortion can lead to a candidate losing the popular vote but winning a majority of the electoral votes, as happened in both 2000 and 2016. The table below shows the distorting effect of the winner-take-all aspect of the Electoral College system in the elections since 2000. The winner's percentage of the electoral votes was more than his popular percentage in every case; minor-party candidates won a small but not insignificant percentage of the total popular vote in some of these elections, notably 2000 (4 percent) and 2016 (6 percent), but won no electoral votes.

To illustrate the distorting effect of the winner-take-all feature of the Electoral College system in the United States, consider the 2004 presidential election. If fewer than 27,000 votes had

Table 10. Popular vote percentage and electoral vote percentage in recent US presidential elections

Year	Winner	Percentage of popular vote	Percentage of electoral vote
2000	George W. Bush	47.9	50.7
2004	George W. Bush	50.7	53.1
2008	Barack Obama	52.9	67.8
2012	Barack Obama	51.1	61.7
2016	Donald Trump	46.0	55.5
2020	Joe Biden	51.3	56.9

switched from George W. Bush to John Kerry in just three states (Iowa, 10,089 votes; New Mexico, 5,988 votes; and Wisconsin, 11,384 votes)—each decided by less than 1 percent of the votes cast—Kerry would have been elected president with 273 electoral votes, instead of the 255 he in fact won. That would have required a switch of only 27,000 votes out of over 121 million cast, approximately 0.02 percent of the votes cast.

Another outcome of electoral systems is government strength, or effectiveness, referring to the stability of governments and their capacity to pass legislation. Government stability is often associated with single-party government, which in turn is likely to arise from elections that produce clear winners. In parliamentary systems with plurality electoral systems, like that of the United Kingdom, single-party governments can typically count on a majority in parliament to support the government's agenda, resulting in a process of making legislation that is expedient and unencumbered by the need to compromise with another party. Plurality electoral systems encourage cooperation before elections; that is, candidates aim to appeal to a broad audience and therefore tend to be moderate. In PR systems, cooperation tends to occur after elections in the process of forming a coalition government. To govern, coalition governments must cooperate and seek consensus, occasionally requiring compromise, which some think may water down or slow down policy change or innovation. Coalition governments that typically arise from PR systems are often considered to be inherently less stable than single-party governments.

Are these perceptions based in reality? Maybe not. Some countries, like the United States, have fixed legislative terms, which make the system appear to be highly stable. Parliamentary systems do not typically have fixed legislative terms, and they do vary in terms of electoral systems, so it is worthwhile to look more comparatively before declaring one system to be inherently more stable.

In fact, countries with PR systems are by many measures as stable or more stable than those with winner-take-all systems. Take the example of Austria, which has a PR electoral system with a relatively low threshold of 4 percent and is among the most stable countries in the world, with governments typically lasting the full legislative term. Measured in terms of length of government duration, countries with plurality/majority systems do appear to be among the most stable in terms of average government duration—so, too, are a number of PR systems, such as Spain, Costa Rica, Colombia, Sweden, and Norway, and mixed electoral systems like those of New Zealand and Germany. Moreover, the composition of governments in parliamentary systems, including the top post of prime minister, can change during a legislative period without triggering new elections, as happened in Great Britain with the resignation of Prime Minister Boris Johnson in 2022. In such cases, the political stability of the country is normally not affected.

A better measure of stability may be the frequency of elections to parliament; the more frequent the elections, the less stable the system is believed to be, since in parliamentary systems, a loss of confidence in a government can trigger new elections. When taking the number of elections during a period of years into account, PR systems actually do a bit better than non-PR systems; among nations of the Organisation for Economic Co-operation and Development (OECD), between 1945 and 1998, PR systems averaged 16.0 elections and plurality/majority systems averaged 16.7.

Finally, the Fragile State Index, which considers 12 measures of stability, found that the more disproportional an electoral system is, the more unstable a country tends to be. One explanation is that coalition governments tend to have more stable policies, including economic policy, while plurality/majority systems are prone to policy lurches when one single-party government is replaced with another with a different policy orientation. It seems that one of the major arguments for plurality/majority systems, government stability, does not hold up. There is no appreciable trade-off between a system that prioritizes proportionality and one that has stable governments.

Electoral systems can affect another aspect of governance—whether there is adversarial and partisan politics or consensus and power-sharing. In presidential and semi-presidential political systems with majoritarian electoral rules, divided government is a possibility, whereby the directly elected president is from one party and the parliamentary majority from another. Such a situation can lead not only to a high degree of partisanship but also to gridlock.

Proportional systems, associated with consensus-seeking governance, might be attractive to countries with divided societies—regionally, ethnically, linguistically, and so on—as a means of bridging divides through inclusion and conciliation. So-called consociational (cooperative, power-sharing) features, like PR, give parties representing minority groups a chance to compete for seats in parliament and, perhaps, to share in executive power through coalition governments. Skeptics contend that PR systems do not bridge divides but rather institutionalize divisions in society by encouraging the existence of many, competitive parties, leading to fragmentation in parliaments, and making it challenging to build stable coalition governments. Belgium is an extreme example of this. Since 1993, when the country changed its constitution to become a federal state, the party system split into two regional variations, one Flemish and one Wallonian, or French-speaking. In the now extremely multiparty system, it is more difficult to build majority governments, often taking many months.

Electoral rules affect the ability of new political parties to emerge and gain seats in legislatures. In plurality and majority systems, new and small parties would need to be concentrated in a district to win a seat. Though that can happen, as in the case of regional parties like Plaid Cymru in Wales, which has support concentrated in some districts, or in the case of green parties in urban areas, such as in the German cities of Berlin, Hamburg, Munich, Frankfurt, and Stuttgart, plurality and majoritarian systems decidedly reward larger, established parties. PR systems, especially those with no or low thresholds for entering parliament and those with large district magnitudes, provide greater opportunity for new parties to emerge and compete in elections. Small parties in PR systems, moreover, can occasionally become "kingmakers," making or breaking a coalition and extracting benefits (such as cabinet posts and policy concessions) that small parties in plurality and majority systems rarely achieve. This has long been true of the small liberal party, the Free Democrats, in Germany, or any number of small parties in Israel whose support is necessary to build majority coalition governments.

The emergence of new parties brings new issues and priorities to the fore and often mobilizes new segments of the electorate. For example, ecology-oriented parties emerged as "new" parties in many Western European PR systems in the 1980s. However, electoral systems with PR and high district magnitude can also facilitate the emergence of radical and extremist parties on the fringes of the political spectrum. Such parties have a harder time winning seats or offices in a winner-take-all system than in a PR or mixed one. The role of ultra-Orthodox parties and—in 2021—of the United Arab List in forming Israeli governments are clear examples of how the low threshold for securing seats in the Knesset gives smaller parties more influence.

Logically, the ease or difficulty experienced by new entrants and the ability of small parties to win seats and participate in governments have implications for the party system in a given country. Single-member district (SMD) systems encourage competition between two dominant parties, as with the US Democrats and Republicans, while systems based on proportionality encourage multiparty competition and multiparty party systems, found in most democracies around the world that were not English colonies. The two-round system (TRS) is associated with two blocs of parties. Small parties need concentrated support to win a majority in the first round of voting in an SMD. Runoffs in TRSs tend to be between candidates from the two dominant parties, so the candidates and supporters of smaller parties will line up behind the candidate that is closest to them ideologically. In French elections, for example, any party on the left that did not proceed to the runoff would support a leftist party, usually the Socialists, in the second round of voting.

Do electoral systems have an impact on public policy or quality of life indicators? Might governance style, whether partisan or consensual, lead to different decisions about public spending? PR systems tend to have higher taxes and higher public spending, meaning greater depth and breadth of social services, than nonproportional electoral systems. The reason for these economic policy effects lies in whom policymakers aim to please—whether a relatively narrow or broad segment of the population. In plurality systems, where elections often lead to a manufactured majority and where two dominant parties are typical, policy is likelier to be targeted to a narrower segment of the electorate, whereas in PR systems, which often have coalition governments, policy should aim to address the concerns and needs of a broader segment of the electorate. Where some element of PR is present in a system, spending on social security and welfare is likely to be higher than in plurality and majoritarian electoral systems; one study found that, on average, the difference is about 8 percent of GDP. When New Zealand switched from a plurality system to a mixed system, social spending increased 2.08 percentage points.

Electoral systems can influence the incentives and behaviors of voters, candidates during election campaigns, and politicians once elected. Whether people believe voting is worth their time and effort can be affected by many features of the electoral system, ranging from the convenience of casting a vote to the degree to which they feel their vote will have an impact on the people who lead and the policies they produce. Majoritarian systems result in "wasted votes," which can lead voters either not to vote at all or to choose a candidate, usually from a dominant party, who is likely to win but not their preferred candidate. PR systems have less distortion; that is, there is less disproportionality between vote share and seat share for a party. Average voter participation in PR systems is higher (9 percentage points higher in one oft-cited study) than in non-PR systems. This difference would suggest that voters understand that aspect of the system and have faith in its integrity.

Mixed electoral systems provide voters with the accountability of a single-member plurality vote and the fairness in representation of PR. It is likely this feature that led experts to rank this type of electoral system highest in a 2004 survey reported by Shaun Bowler and David Farrell, and it is likely why several post-Communist democracies chose mixed electoral systems in the early 1990s, and why New Zealand switched from plurality to a mixed system in 1993. Voters in mixed systems, particularly linked systems like the mixed-member proportional (MMP) system in Germany, allow voters to split their votes and vote strategically: they can give their plurality vote to their favored candidate of their favored party and their PR vote to the smaller party that would be a fitting coalition partner to their preferred party. When voters have a choice, either to rank candidates, such as in preferential voting systems, or to change the order of candidates on an open party list in a PR system, they may be more inclined to vote. In other words, the electoral system gives voters an increased sense of political efficacy, increasing their motivation to vote. For its combination of multimember district PR and voter choice via ranking of candidates, single transferable vote (STV) came in second in the expert survey of electoral systems.

Certainly other features of elections influence voters' perceptions and behaviors, although the magnitude of the effects is difficult to measure. Where voter registration is automatic or easy—and certainly where voting is compulsory—turnout in elections will be greater. There is little evidence that greater access to voting compromises the security of the ballot. What is clear, though, is that the issue of election security is often politicized by candidates or political parties that seek to limit access as a strategy for retaining their electoral advantage. The most obvious example of this is in the United States, where the "Stop the Steal" conspiracy theory fomented by Donald Trump after the 2020 election caught on in right-wing state legislatures, leading to the imposition of new restrictions on voter registration.

The administration of elections by nonpartisan election management bodies (EMBs) is a global trend with a number of positive outcomes, such as fair and consistent voter registration and nonpartisan drawing of electoral districts. EMBs also typically provide impartial information about the voting process and about candidates and parties competing for office. The result of such

10. On November 14, 2020, crowds at a "Voter Fraud" rally marched to the US Supreme Court in support of Donald Trump, who refused to concede the election.

efforts is likely to be a better-informed electorate and, potentially, higher levels of participation in elections. It is difficult to ascertain the impact of electoral system features on voters' trust. Public opinion surveys tend not to ask questions about specific elements of electoral systems and rules, since the commonly held assumption is that most voters do not understand them or have only a very general understanding of them. It stands to reason that when elections run smoothly and efficiently, including the processes of registration, dissemination of unbiased information about the issues and candidates, the casting of votes, and the counting of those votes, then public trust in elections will be positively affected.

The campaign that precedes an election is another opportunity for increasing voter awareness and interest in participating in the democratic process. Most people would agree that fairness and transparency are qualities that elections should exhibit. Where election campaigns drag on for many months, as in the United States, and when the airwaves and Internet are saturated with campaign ads, particularly negative ones, voter fatigue is likelier. State funding of campaigns, another feature of many elections outside of the United States, helps ensure that smaller parties have fairer access to campaign resources, and it allows incumbents to focus on their legislative or executive work rather than raising money for the next campaign.

Electoral rules may also incentivize candidates to behave in certain ways. Whether candidates depend on voters or their party to further their career influences their appeals during election campaigns, whether to their own party, to the general electorate, or to voters in their own district. Candidates in SMD systems, such as the plurality system or the majoritarian TRS, are more likely to engage in personalized versus party-centered campaigns. In the United States, candidate-centered campaigns increasingly "go negative," using highly targeted attack ads. This happens far less frequently in other plurality/majority systems where campaign rules and/or cultural norms prohibit such negative tactics.

Once officials are elected, do electoral systems affect their perceptions and behaviors? Legislators elected by PR view their role as a partisan, as someone who represents their party's principles and goals. It is the party, after all, that decides whether individual candidates appear on the party list at election time and how high or low on the list they appear, affecting their chance of being elected, and also reflecting their status in the party. Officials who won SMD seats may view their role as a delegate of their district. The electoral system, then, affects politicians' calculations about policy choices—whether they should align with their party or their electorate. Finally, representatives with district mandates may be more likely than those with list mandates to focus on constituency work, since they have a home district and are more likely to feel pressure to respond to it, particularly in an election cycle.

It may be that the effects of electoral rules are magnified or diminished by context-specific factors. Longer-term developments, such as the length of time a country has been a democracy or the nature and severity of divides in society, may impact the electoral system's effects on political behavior or on other institutions. More immediate contextual factors, such as whether an election is seen as having high stakes, or whether there are negative environmental factors, such as manipulation of the rules, disinformation, or strains on the political system caused by shocks, would also be expected to affect voter behavior. Certainly the integrity of elections in a globalized, high-tech environment presents new challenges to voters, candidates, and election officials. Another trend that has affected and will continue to affect electoral systems is the demand for greater access to voting and greater inclusivity of candidates and officials from traditionally marginalized groups. The demographic representation of elected bodies is increasingly a concern in many countries, whether old or new democracies.

Chapter 6

Reforming electoral systems: values and priorities

Elections around the world do not always garner attention outside of the country holding them, but a number of recent ones have illustrated the consequences of electoral systems and rules in stunning ways. Among the democratic countries listed in tables in this volume, Israel is notable for holding five elections in four years, bringing Benjamin Netanyahu back to power in 2022, this time in a government with extreme right-wing parties. The Israeli system elects all 120 seats in the Knesset with closed-list proportional representation (PR) in a single nationwide constituency with a 3.25 percent threshold. That means that party leaders have a great deal of control over who is put on the party list, and thus who is likely to be seated in parliament. The single constituency and PR system with a low bar for entry into parliament result in many parties being represented in the legislature, making coalition-building challenging, and often bringing small, fringe parties into government that then wield greater power than their numbers would suggest. Beyond these electoral system features, it is noteworthy that in the occupied territories, only Israeli settlers are allowed to vote in Knesset elections.

In early 2023, Nigeria held a presidential election under a new Electoral Act, enacted the year before to make elections more secure and transparent. Many observers lauded the election for being the most competitive in years and for the role of civil society and the media in the run-up to the election; however, others criticized the elections for delays in tallying the vote; incidents of violence, including attacks on election officials; and rampant disinformation that cast doubt on the integrity of the vote. Bola Tinubu of the governing All Progressives Congress party was declared the winner, since he met the required thresholds for victory: a plurality of the national vote with 35.3 percent, and over 25 percent of the vote in two-thirds of Nigeria's 36 states. Some opposition parties called for a rerun of the election, which a court dismissed. While outside observers recognized Tinubu as the winner and praised the country's efforts to safeguard fair elections, it is telling that of the 94 million registered voters in Nigeria, of whom 87 million received voting cards making them eligible to vote, only 27 million did so.

Elections matter, and so, too, do their rules and system features. The variety of elections is bewildering, and that variety begs the question: Is there a model system of elections? There is no one-size-fits-all formula for how elections should be run; historical, cultural, and demographic context matter. Democratic elections reflect certain core values. What are those values? What electoral processes reflect them? What steps can be taken to realize them—and what constraints prevent countries from taking those steps?

Various organizations, such as the ACE (Administration and Cost of Elections) Electoral Knowledge Network, International IDEA (Institute for Democracy and Electoral Assistance), and Freedom House, have defined values that characterize a properly functioning electoral system in a democracy. Defining those values is actually not difficult. A properly functioning electoral system should be fair to all candidates. In particular, all candidates should have an equal opportunity to run for office, to make their case to the electorate, and to have their votes counted accurately. Their supporters should be permitted to campaign on their behalf and have equal access to the polls.

Similarly, an ideal electoral system should be open to all participants. That is, those who want to participate—as candidates, as interested parties, or as voters—should not be prohibited, by law or extralegal means, from full and effective participation. Those interested in affecting the outcome of an election should have the opportunity to do so.

The electoral process should be transparent. Citizens should know what offices are on the ballot, who is running for which offices, when and where they are to cast their ballots, and by what means they are to do so. They should also know who is running the election, how the votes are to be tallied, and by whom. The results should be communicated clearly and in a timely manner. Avenues for challenging the reported results should be well known to all. Citizens should feel that the integrity of the entire process is unquestioned. They should believe in their electoral system—that it is not corrupt, and that it is fair, open, and transparent.

These are clear and quite obvious principles. But is their meaning really so evident? For example, in many countries, citizens must return to the municipality where they first registered to vote in order to exercise the franchise. Are those systems then equally open to all citizens? In many countries, parties must demonstrate a level of support, such as attaining a threshold of signatures or supporters or money raised, in order to secure a place on the ballot. Is that fair to all candidates? If it is possible for those in government to establish a threshold, for what we may agree are legitimate purposes, can that power not be abused—by setting those thresholds so high that new entrants into politics cannot reach them, for instance? If a rule can be abused by those in power, does its mere existence violate a basic principle of fairness?

If the principles of fairness, openness, and transparency can be subject to interpretation, is that not even more the case for the principle of representativeness? Certainly a basic value for an effective electoral system is that the results of an election should reflect the views of the voters. If the ultimate goal of an electoral process is to allow the citizenry to express their views on the issues of the day through the actions of their elected representatives, those elected should have views that reflect those of the voters. But how closely? Through what mechanism? Is it necessary for candidates and parties to run on well-defined platforms, and to legislate according to those platforms if they attain power? Should representative assemblies reflect just the views of the voters, or should they reflect the demographic composition of the electorate as well? Should the views of citizens in geographic regions of a country be represented, or only views of the country as a whole? If legislators accurately reflect the views of their constituents but are unable to enact legislation because of constraints imposed by governmental institutions, protections for minority views as an example, does that imply that the electoral system fails to meet the principle of representation?

None of these questions yields an easy answer, but each is fundamental to assessing how effectively electoral systems and elections work. The easiest answers are found when basic principles are violated. If an opposition leader is prevented from running for office, as in Nicaragua or Venezuela in recent elections, or from campaigning openly and publicly, as in Guatemala's 2023 election, the electoral system fails the basic test of fairness. If citizens are prevented from voting because of their race or economic status, the system fails the basic test of openness. If legislative seats are apportioned in such a way that whole regions are essentially disenfranchised, as was the case in the United States before the apportioning standard of one-person, one-vote was established in the 1960s, the system fails the basic test of representation. So, too, one might argue, does the US Senate, in which the senators from Alaska each represent about 750,000 people while those from California each represent 39,500,000 residents.

But what of the more difficult, less clear cases? Are some of the processes of apportioning seats, choosing candidates, determining winners, and administering elections essentially better than others for creating an electoral system that reflects the basic values of democracy?

Prioritizing reforms to reflect values

Let's start with the low-hanging fruit. Election management bodies (EMBs), when effective, are nonpartisan, professional bureaucracies established for the purpose of assuring that elections held in a country meet the basic values. They establish uniform procedures for an election, apply them in an unbiased manner, and inform all participants—activists and average citizens—of those procedures.

EMBs are often responsible for determining who is eligible to vote, maintaining the roster of eligible voters, assuring that all eligible voters are afforded the opportunity to vote, and overseeing the casting of ballots. They set the standards for candidate or party eligibility and apply those standards in a fair way. In many cases, they are responsible for providing basic information about the candidates to the electorate, again in a manner that is even and fair to all candidates. Most often EMBs oversee the counting of the votes and report and certify the results of elections. Leaders of these organizations are most often appointed—often for rather long terms—by government officials who cut across the party or ideological divisions in a country. Again, though this practice is not universal, most EMB leaders are not partisans and have experience and credentials that are appropriate to managing a countrywide electoral process. Their unbiased, professional actions in this role add legitimacy to the electoral process.

Residents of countries with respected and effective EMBs—Costa Rica and Germany, for example—would question why it is necessary to state something so obvious. Residents of countries whose election administration is questioned—such as the Philippines, Serbia, or Turkmenistan, and other often-failed or failing democracies—would have a very different response, thinking how good it would be if they trusted those running elections to do so fairly. And residents of the United States would marvel that countries have only one EMB, since each American state has its own, often very partisan, set of officials charged with managing elections.

And therein lies the problem. What seems like a relatively simple, effective reform on its face seems beyond the reach of those in many countries. But difficulty in achieving a reform, particularly one that is balanced and, if managed correctly, nonpolitical, should not preclude the effort to attempt to attain it.

Similar cases can be made for reforms that implement universal suffrage in a fair way. While there are philosophical reasons to oppose compulsory voting, similar objections cannot be raised about affording every citizen ease of access to voting. In the United States, failure to register is the single largest roadblock to voting. In countries such as Sweden or Australia, where the state is responsible for adding citizens to the voting rolls once they reach the minimum age required to vote, that roadblock does not exist. Voting—the act of participating in the decision of who should govern—is a right, not a privilege. The state should guarantee that right.

Again, the response to this notion varies by the residence of who is responding. Citizens in countries that use automatic registration think it is obvious and easy. To citizens in other countries, it is not so clear. Some have claimed, particularly in recent years, that fraud will enter into politics, that those not eligible to vote will do so. Although avoiding corruption in the electoral process is a value everyone espouses, there is scant evidence of fraud in any of the countries with universal registration; those in the United States who claim that ease of access to the voting rolls will lead to fraud have failed to produce any evidence to back their claim. While paper vote lists were easily corrupted in the early twentieth century, technological advances make this reform all the more appealing.

Failure to register is the single reason that keeps most nonvoters from the polls. However, requiring citizens to vote at a particular place at a particular (often limited) time also discourages citizens from exercising the franchise. Voting should be made as easy as possible for citizens; extra administrative expense should not be an excuse for keeping anyone from the polls. Well-regulated systems of early voting or absentee voting meet the basic criteria for an effective electoral process. Citizens voting at one place at one time is a relic from an earlier time when such a system was necessary to guarantee the values we seek to achieve. But long experience with absentee voting has proven its effectiveness in opening the process to those who cannot be at the designated polling place on Election Day. Early voting in many places has been equally effective. We know of no value-based objection to these practices, though some do oppose them for clearly political reasons. Further reform, such as online voting, may be appropriate to ease access to the polls, but these two reforms, allowing absentee voting and early voting, could be implemented by any democracy seeking to increase voter turnout—without compromising any other agreed-upon values.

Effective electoral systems are those in which basic information is provided to the citizenry in a nonbiased, easily understood, and timely manner. This goal can be accomplished in any number of ways. It could, but need not, be provided by the government, through an election management function, but that would not preclude others "informing" the electorate through private means. The principle is clear: citizens should be informed about what parties and what individual candidates stand for and what their priorities are. Many nations restrict the period of time over which parties and candidates can campaign. Such restrictions might work to avoid information overload, but the basic principle is that information should reach the electorate in an unbiased manner. Increasingly, citizens receive false information about upcoming elections from various sources seeking to influence election results. Artificial intelligence has made disinformation campaigns easier and more prevalent. As a consequence, effective electoral systems must come up with a means to ferret out and combat this type of false electioneering.

The more controversial questions about electoral system reform involve the trade-offs between plurality/majoritarian systems and proportional systems. To be sure, there are models in between these two. The single transferrable vote (STV) model used in Ireland is one such voting method favored by many reformers. While the Irish seem comfortable with STV, others feel it is too complex for widespread adoption. From a purely representational point of view, PR is preferred—unless one is concerned about subnational geographic representation. The degree to which the representational function of elections is served in single-member districts (which privilege geographic representation) can be enhanced by reform in voting systems. For instance, preferential voting (PV), known as ranked choice voting (RCV) in the United States, allows citizens to express their preference for the type of representative who serves them far more accurately than does a plurality system, and it produces a winner with the support of a majority of voters.

In addition, the representational questions of a majoritarian system versus a proportional system are often confounded by other institutional rules, such as the clearly non-majoritarian Electoral College used to elect presidents of the United States. That system has enabled a winner—in a supposed majoritarian system—with fewer voters than the loser in two of the six presidential elections between 2000 and 2020. Systems that claim to be majoritarian are often dominated by minority factions when it comes to converting electoral majorities to legislative action. For example, a party that controls a majority of seats in the US Senate cannot convert that majority status into desired legislation because the Senate has procedural rules that require 60 votes to pass many types of legislation. Thus, while a majority of the elected US senators might favor passage of a restriction on the sale of semiautomatic weapons, that preference cannot be translated into law because of legislative procedures that require a supermajority before passage can be achieved.

Too often, these questions are not asked or examined in depth; instead, the existing system is merely accepted as the only alternative. The goal is not so much that any existing system be changed, but rather that policymakers and reformers think comparatively and critically about the system under which they function. Fundamental national reforms to electoral systems are rare, but not unheard of.

Fundamental electoral system reform

Changing the fundamental rules of the game is rarely easy, particularly when the vested interests of powerful political actors are at stake. There are rare occasions when an abrupt opening for reform occurs, as it did in Eastern Europe in the late 1980s, when Communist governments gave way to peaceful transitions to democratic elections. More typically in democratic settings, pressures for reform build over time. In recent decades, scholars and voters have become more attentive to issues of fairness, openness, transparency, and representativeness; and in some cases, policymakers have heeded those concerns and enacted reforms.

All of the new democracies that emerged from decades of Communist, one-party rule, in Eastern Europe in the 1990s chose electoral systems with some element of PR. What about reforms in older democracies? In two established democracies, efforts to reform their plurality systems illustrate both opportunities and constraints inherent in such processes. The first was New Zealand in 1996, which was a case of reform success. The second was the United Kingdom, which tried first in 1997 and then 2011 to reform its system, ending both times in failure.

As a former colony of Britain, New Zealand used the plurality, first-past-the-post (FPTP) system for most of its history. Debate about electoral system reform began in the 1970s and focused significantly on the disproportional nature of FPTP and the possibility of dramatic shifts in policy when one single-party government replaced another. More than one commission examined various electoral system models and recommended a mixed-member proportional (MMP) system, like Germany's, but change was elusive until various systems were put to a nonbinding referendum in 1992. In the run-up to the referendum, a government panel carried out a thorough voter education campaign, sending information about each of the models to every household and using television and face-to-face meetings to inform the public about the choices. In the two-part referendum, 85 percent rejected the FPTP system in question one, and 65 percent chose MMP out of four possible models in question two. A binding referendum followed the next year and was, significantly, held at the same time as a general election. This time, many politicians and business leaders campaigned against the reform, and the outcome was much closer: 53.9 percent of voters chose MMP.

The new system was first used in the 1996 election. In that election, the dominant National Party won 35 percent of the national vote, giving it 44 out of 120 seats, whereas in the 1993 election held under FPTP, the National Party also won 35 percent of the vote but was able to form a majority government. Moreover, in 1996, six parties won seats in parliament, compared to the four parties that won seats in 1993. Thus the new MMP system succeeded in decreasing distortion and increasing proportionality, and it resulted in a legislature that was more accessible to a variety of political parties. Māori representation has more than tripled since the new system was introduced.

The National Party promised another referendum on the electoral system in its 2008 parliamentary campaign. Subsequently, in the 2011 referendum, voters confirmed their preference for MMP—by four percentage points more than in 1993. This story illustrates that changing the election system is not easy and requires public awareness of and support for the change. If enacted, such reforms can have immediate consequences for democratic representation and trust.

The UK system of FPTP has historically benefitted the two largest parties, the Conservatives and Labour, and has disadvantaged small parties. Despite that, new and small parties have appeared, and a few have persisted over time, usually by concentrating their vote share in particular geographic regions. Not surprisingly, these smaller parties have been most enthusiastic about moving away from a plurality system, though they are rarely in a position—in Parliament and, even more rarely, in government—to effect such change.

The first reform effort came about after the Conservative Party's long, 18-year period of governing that ran through the 1980s and most of the 1990s. When Tony Blair assumed the leadership of the Labour Party, he sought to modernize the party and the country, and in doing so, he made a number of campaign promises to reform elements of the antiquated and undemocratic British political system, including the hereditary peerage system of the House of Lords and the FPTP electoral system for the House of Commons. Upon winning the 1997 election, the new Blair government established a commission to examine electoral system models and to recommend the best electoral system for the UK. The Independent Commission on Voting Rights recommended an MMP system, like New Zealand's, but important components of the Labour Party, including members of the cabinet, opposed an MMP system; once in power, they did not want to change electoral rules in ways that might not benefit them. Blair, seemingly obligated by his earlier promise, instead proposed the preferential "alternative vote" (AV) system, which is not based on PR but at least gives the voter the option of ranking candidates for their single-member constituency elections. That proposal, however, also failed to persuade key factions of the party, so the electoral system reform effort was dropped.

The next time reform of the system was proposed, almost a decade and a half later, it was the result of a highly unusual election result, where no party won enough seats to form a government—even with the distortion in votes-to-seats that typically gives a bonus to the plurality winner. In this case, the plurality winner, the Conservatives, formed a coalition with the Liberal Democrats, a party that had long favored an institutional reform agenda that prioritized electoral system change. Because the Conservatives needed the Liberal Democrats' support in order to govern, they conceded to holding a referendum on introducing the AV system for House of Commons elections. Agreeing to a referendum, though, did not mean the Conservatives supported the idea. The outcome of the 2011 referendum was a resounding defeat: only 32.1 percent of voters were in favor of AV.

Interestingly, polls in recent years find that opposition to electoral system reform has softened. A YouGov poll tracking British attitudes between November 2019 and March 2022 found steady support for PR at 44 percent, while far fewer, only 25 percent, favored FPTP. One can imagine the Liberal Democrats and the Greens favoring reform in the future. The question is whether Labour will once again side with the forces of electoral system reform. The chances of this would likely be greatest if Labour found itself in a coalition government with a smaller party—or two.

The factor that seemed to make the difference in New Zealand's reform efforts was its relatively longer and more public debate about reform. People in New Zealand seemed to be more aware of, and more dissatisfied with, the ways the FPTP system affected their society, whereby two large parties benefited at the expense of smaller ones, and single-party majority governments were able to enact policies with less than a majority of the electorate's support. The vested interests in New Zealand may not have favored a change that would threaten their built-in advantage, but they did agree to hold referenda and, before that, to engage in a voter education campaign.

Why so few reforms?

Why have so few other FPTP systems embarked on reform movements? It could be that many people still prefer to prioritize geographic representation over other types of representation. They may still believe the outdated claim that FPTP results in more stable governments than PR-based systems with coalition governments. Or, more likely, they may not have spent much time exploring the advantages and disadvantages of various types of systems.

The kind of fundamental electoral process reform adopted in New Zealand and attempted in the United Kingdom required legislative action, whereas other countries' electoral systems may require constitutional amendment. In the United States, the states' control over the time, manner, and place of elections, specified in Article I of the US Constitution, can be overridden by congressional action. However, more fundamental changes, such as abolishing the Electoral College or apportioning the Senate based on population, not states, would require amendments that seem impossible to enact.

Short of fundamental electoral system reform, there are many improvements that can be made to existing rules guiding election processes. Why are these improvements, relating to uniform administrative bodies, easier registration, or more accessible means of voting, for instance, not more universally adopted? Why is the system in the United States marked by so many obvious areas in which the fundamental values that should mark a democratic electoral process are missing? Why are Americans not concerned that the United States ranks so low on internationally accepted standards of electoral integrity, especially as so many concerned were raised after the 2020 election?

In the United States, amending the Constitution requires the approval of two-thirds of the members of each house of the Congress and of three-quarters of the states, the very entities that would lose the most power were fundamental reforms to the apportionment of the Senate or the election of the president to be passed. Without these reforms, it is difficult to see how the United States could move toward a system that would guarantee that the candidate with the most votes became president, or toward a uniform system of election management, because often the states with the least democratic electoral systems are the small states that control power in the Senate far in excess of what would be a proportional reflection of their population. This dilemma reflects a fundamental lesson of political reform: if those in power favor the status quo, they are unlikely to permit political reform.

Even short of that reform, other changes to reflect best practices in other countries are often difficult to achieve in the United States. The strength of and loyalty to subnational state power in the US federal system impedes most fundamental reform. This attachment to state power is combined with legislative rules that make it impossible to change electoral laws without supermajorities in the Senate, a body in which the power of small states is so evident. Creating one national system for registering voters, regulating the polls, and monitoring elections would be all but impossible to pass through the Senate. Senators and citizens in relatively small, often southern or mountain states, fear that reforms put forth by those from larger, eastern or far western states would be intended to benefit voters in those states. Any reforms proposed by the Democrats controlling New England and the West Coast would automatically be viewed as suspicious by Republicans in the South or the Midwest. In part this is a result of the legacy of electoral reforms put forth during the civil rights era of the 1960s, and in part it reflects the extreme polarization of the United States today. What the Democrats favor, the Republicans oppose; and the opposite is also true. What reformers see as reflecting basic values, politicians view through a partisan lens. Yet these are the exact steps that would move the US toward an electoral process that more closely reflected the values that the country professes to uphold.

But reformers in the United States have paid attention to rules that foster fairness, openness, and transparency in other countries' democratic elections. FairVote, a nonpartisan reform organization, formerly known as the Center for Voting and Democracy, has led many of these efforts, compiling empirical reports on the effects of reform efforts in US cities and states and demonstrating how those efforts led to fairer representation. Their efforts to implement the preferential Ranked Choice Voting (RCV) have resulted in slow but steady progress. RCV, first used for statewide elections in Maine in 2018, has since been adopted for all or some statewide offices in six additional states and for some or all local offices in an additional eleven states.

Others are working toward reform of the Electoral College system, seeking changes in how the system is implemented even if repeal is not likely in the foreseeable future. Nearly half of the US states have altered the process through which legislative lines are drawn, removing the process from the control of state legislators and putting it into the hands of independent commissions or judges. These and other steps demonstrate a consciousness that the US claim to be a model for democracy for the world is falling short.

Finding solutions to some problems with how elections are run throughout the world is an ongoing problem of adaptation to how citizens live and learn. Once all electioneering was person-to-person and the torch-lit parade was the campaign technique most often used. Candidates rarely traveled far from their home base. But technological changes led to new ways of campaigning. Advances in rail travel made it easier for candidates to see more voters. Radio and then television made it possible for candidates to air their messages far and wide. Air travel led to cross-country campaign swings in a matter of days. Advances in computing made it possible for campaign organizations to segment the population and target appeals for votes and for money. Social media transformed the ways in which candidates and campaigns communicated with their followers and recruited new adherents. Artificial intelligence will take campaign communications to uncharted territory.

New media bring greater opportunities for campaign communication, but they also bring greater opportunities for abuse. Disinformation campaigns have challenged elections around the globe. The attack on the United States Capitol in January 2021 and the fact that so many Americans—including a majority of Republicans—appear to believe President Trump's Big Lie that the election was stolen suggest that voter education and trust in elections require careful attention, even in the most established of democracies.

In some cases, countries have adopted laws to respond to changes in political communication: some restrict political adverting on television, and some differ between commercial and public television in terms of regulation. But in many others, campaign techniques have evolved to incorporate these technological changes; narrowcasting to specific audiences on social media is an example of such adaptation. In countries with guaranteed free speech, especially with an emphasis on guaranteed free political speech, it is difficult to restrict how candidates and parties reach the electorate, but norms often restrict intrusive campaign tactics. Even within one country—and certainly when comparing countries—campaign tactics that are acceptable in one place would be counterproductive in another. To be blunt, American-style negative campaigning can be exported to some democracies—Israel or Brazil might be examples—but would be frowned upon in others—such as Germany or Japan.

One cannot overestimate the challenges that an evolving campaign environment presents to those dedicated to free, fair, open, and transparent campaigns. But the work of democracy is often difficult. Citizens must be aware of the flaws in their own system, not view it as above reproach. Nowhere is this more true than in the United States, whose citizens claim it to be the most admired democracy in the world while its election system fails the most basic tests of how a democracy should function. What we look for is an effort to keep basic democratic values in mind as countries deal with changing campaign techniques in an evolving electoral environment—and that is the work that reformers have taken as their mission since the spread of democracies.

Further reading

General online resources

ACE Electoral Knowledge Network (https://aceproject.org/about-en/) is an extensive online resource covering a broad variety of topics related to electoral processes across the globe. It features information about elections in specific countries, an extensive database of comparative election data, a virtual collection of election materials, and much more.

The Electoral Integrity Project (https://www.electoralintegrityproject. com/) compares elections worldwide, focusing on failed elections and electoral reforms.

The Fund for Peace, Fragile State Index, Global Data measures vulnerabilities that contribute to state collapse. The Index includes 178 countries (https://fragilestatesindex.org/global-data/).

The International Institute for Democracy and Electoral Assistance (https://www.idea.int/theme/electoral-processes) is an intergovernmental institution featuring several work streams for promoting democracy worldwide, including one on electoral processes. It offers a wide variety of publications and tools to promote good electoral processes.

V-Dem, Varieties of Democracy (https://v-dem.net/) is a data set measuring democracy along five principles, one of which is electoral.

Role of elections in democracies

Boese-Schlosser, Vanessa Alexandra, Nazifa Alizada, Martin Lundstedt, Kelly Morrison, Natalia Natsika, Yuko Sato, Hugo Tai, and Staffan Lindberg. "Autocratization Changing Nature? Democracy Report 2022." Varieties of Democracy Institute (V-Dem), 2002. Available at https://ssrn.com/abstract=4052548 or http://dx.doi.org/10.2139/ssrn.4052548.

Diamond, Larry, and Marc F. Plattner, eds. *Electoral Systems and Democracy*. Baltimore: Johns Hopkins University Press, 2006.

Maisel, L. Sandy, and Mark Brewer. *Parties and Elections in America: The Electoral Process*. 9th ed. Lanham, MD: Rowman & Littlefield, 2020.

Electoral system types

Amy, Douglas J. "PR Library: A Brief History of Proportional Representation in the United States." Fair Vote. https://fairvote.org/archives/a-brief-history-of-proportional-representation-in-the-united-states/.

Bowler, Shaun, and David Farrell. "We Know Which One We Prefer, But We Don't Really Know Why: The Curious Case of Mixed Member Electoral Systems." *British Journal of Politics and International Relations* 8, no. 3 (2006): 445–60.

Farrell, David M. *Electoral Systems: A Comparative Introduction*. 2nd ed. Basingstoke, UK: Palgrave Macmillan, 2011.

Herron, Erik S., Robert J. Pekkanen, and Matthew S. Shugart, eds. *The Oxford Handbook of Electoral Systems*. New York: Oxford University Press, 2018.

Impacts of election rules

Achen, Christopher H., and Larry M. Bartels. *Democracy for Realists: Why Elections Do Not Produce Responsive Government*. Princeton, NJ: Princeton University Press, 2017.

Fair Vote Canada. "Proportional Representation and Stability: Fact Check." https://www.fairvote.ca/factcheckstability/.

Kaid, Lynda Lee, and Christina Holtz-Bacha, eds. *The Sage Handbook of Political Advertising*. Beverly Hills, CA: Sage, 2006.

Lijphart, Arend. *Electoral Systems and Party Systems: A Study of Twenty-Seven Democracies, 1945–1990*. New York: Oxford University Press, 1991.

Persson, Torsten, and Guido Tabellini. "Electoral Systems and Economic Policy." In *The Oxford Handbook of Political Economy*, edited by Barry R. Weingast and Donald A. Wittman, 723–38. New York: Oxford University Press, 2006.

Profeta, Paola, and Eleanor Florence Woodhouse. "Do Electoral Rules Matter for Female Representation?" CESifo Working Paper Series No. 7101. Munich: CESifo International Research Network, 2018. Available at https://ssrn.com/abstract=3228372 or http://dx.doi.org/10.2139/ssrn.3228372.

Voting

Fiorina, Morris P. *Retrospective Voting in American National Elections*. New Haven, CT: Yale University Press, 1981.

Key, V. O., Jr., with Milton C. Cummings. *The Responsible Electorate: Rationality in Presidential Voting, 1936–1960*. Cambridge, MA: Harvard University Press, 1964.

Solijonev, Abdurashid. *Voter Turnout Trends and the World*. Stockholm: International Institute for Democracy and Electoral Assistance, 2016. idea.int/publlications/catalogue/voter-turnout-trends-around-world.

Uggen, Christopher, Ryan Larson, Sarah Shannon, and Robert Stewart. "Locked Out 2022: Estimates of People Denied Voting Rights." The Sentencing Project, October 25, 2022. https://www.sentencingproject.org/reports/locked-out-2022-estimates-of-people-denied-voting-rights/.

Election reform

Bowler, Shaun, and Todd Donovan. *The Limits of Electoral Reform*. New York: Oxford University Press, 2013.

James, Toby. "Elections: A Global Ranking Rates US Weakest among Liberal Democracies." Kingston, ON: Electoral Integrity Project, June 13, 2022. https://www.electoralintegrityproject.com/eip-blog/2022/6/13/plxw8zwd4m7thgurqvyqdj6qjhyhjw.

Renwick, Alan. *The Politics of Electoral Reform: Changing the Rules of Democracy*. New York: Cambridge University Press, 2010.

Santucci, Jack. *More Parties or No Parties: The Politics of Electoral Reform in America*. New York: Oxford University Press, 2022.

Vowles, Jack. "Electoral Systems in Context: New Zealand." In *The Oxford Handbook of Electoral Systems*, edited by Erik S. Herron, Robert J. Pekkanen, and Matthew S. Shugart, 805–24. New York: Oxford University Press, 2018.

Index

Note: Tables and figures are indicated by an italic "*t*" and "*f*", respectively, following the page number.

For the benefit of digital users, indexed terms that span two pages (e.g., 52–53) may, on occasion, appear on only one of those pages.

W

ARISTOCRACY
A Very Short Introduction
William Doyle

This short introduction shows how ideas of aristocracy originated in ancient times, were transformed in the Middle Ages, and have only fallen apart over the last two centuries. The myths in which aristocracies have always sought to shroud themselves are stripped away, but the true sources of their enduring power are also revealed. Their outlook and behaviour affected the rest of society in innumerable and sometimes surprising ways, but perhaps most surprising was the way in which a centuries-old aristocratic hegemony crumbled away over the last two hundred years. In this *Very Short Introduction* William Doyle considers why this happened and what remains today.

www.oup.com/vsi

BEHAVIOURAL ECONOMICS
A Very Short Introduction
Michelle Baddeley

Traditionally economists have based their economic predictions on the assumption that humans are super-rational creatures, using the information we are given efficiently and generally making selfish decisions that work well for us as individuals. Economists also assume that we're doing the very best we can possibly do—not only for today, but over our whole lifetimes too. Increasingly, however, the study of behavioural economics is revealing that our lives are not that simple. Instead, our decisions are complicated by our own psychology. Each of us makes mistakes every day. We don't always know what's best for us and, even if we do, we might not have the self-control to deliver on our best intentions. We struggle to stay on diets, to get enough exercise, and to manage our money.

This *Very Short Introduction* explores the reasons why we make irrational decisions; how we decide quickly; why we make mistakes in risky situations; our tendency to procrastinate; and how we are affected by social influences, personality, mood, and emotions. As Michelle Baddeley explains, the implications of understanding the rationale for our own financial behaviour are huge. She concludes by looking forward, to see what the future of behavioural economics holds for us.

FREE SPEECH
A Very Short Introduction
Nigel Warburton

'I disapprove of what you say, but I will defend to the death your right to say it' This slogan, attributed to Voltaire, is frequently quoted by defenders of free speech. Yet it is rare to find anyone prepared to defend all expression in every circumstance, especially if the views expressed incite violence. So where do the limits lie? What is the real value of free speech? Here, Nigel Warburton offers a concise guide to important questions facing modern society about the value and limits of free speech: Where should a civilized society draw the line? Should we be free to offend other people's religion? Are there good grounds for censoring pornography? Has the Internet changed everything? This Very Short Introduction is a thought-provoking, accessible, and up-to-date examination of the liberal assumption that free speech is worth preserving at any cost.

'The genius of Nigel Warburton's *Free Speech* lies not only in its extraordinary clarity and incisiveness. Just as important is the way Warburton addresses freedom of speech - and attempts to stifle it - as an issue for the 21st century. More than ever, we need this book.'

Denis Dutton, University of Canterbury, New Zealand

FUNDAMENTALISM
A Very Short Introduction
Malise Ruthven

Malise Ruthven tackles the polemic and stereotypes surrounding this complex phenomenon - one that eludes him today, a conclusion impossible to ignore since the events in New York on September 11 2001. But what does 'fundamentalism' really mean? Since it was coined by American Protestant evangelicals in the 1920s, the use of the term 'fundamentalist' has expanded to include a diverse range of radical conservatives and ideological purists, not all religious. Ruthven investigates fundamentalism's historical, social, religious, political, and ideological roots, and tackles the polemic and stereotypes surrounding this complex phenomenon - one that eludes simple definition, yet urgently needs to be understood.

' . . . powerful stuff . . . this book is perceptive and important.'

Observer

STATISTICS
A Very Short Introduction
David J. Hand

Modern statistics is very different from the dry and dusty discipline of the popular imagination. In its place is an exciting subject which uses deep theory and powerful software tools to shed light and enable understanding. And it sheds this light on all aspects of our lives, enabling astronomers to explore the origins of the universe, archaeologists to investigate ancient civilisations, governments to understand how to benefit and improve society, and businesses to learn how best to provide goods and services. Aimed at readers with no prior mathematical knowledge, this *Very Short Introduction* explores and explains how statistics work, and how we can decipher them.

www.oup.com/vsi